Becoming a
Grand Champion Church

Exploring the Twenty-Third Psalm as a
Blueprint for Church Growth

DALE HEINOLD

WESTBOW
P R E S S
A DIVISION OF THOMAS NELSON

WestBow Press books may be ordered through booksellers or by contacting:

WestBow Press
A Division of Thomas Nelson
1663 Liberty Drive
Bloomington, IN 47403
www.westbowpress.com
1-(866) 928-1240

ISBN: 978-1-4497-4147-1 (hc)
ISBN: 978-1-4497-4146-4 (sc)
ISBN: 978-1-4497-4145-7 (e)

Library of Congress Control Number: 2012903232

Printed in the United States of America

WestBow Press rev. date: 03/06/2012

CONTENTS

This work is dedicated to the memory of my mom,
Judy Heinold.
You shepherded your "lambs" well through life,
and we miss your caring love.

FORWARD

Dear Friends,

In today's busy life, we can find ourselves so rushed. Many passages of God's Word bring us back to a much-needed reflection of the sovereignty of God. Psalm 23 is one such passage. The author uses this passage to bring us to a place where we can almost smell the fresh air and see the barn and pasture. We can hear the sheep as they respond to being feed and cared for even when they are not fully cooperating with their caretaker. The author's insight into the twenty-third psalm will help bring you closer to Christ likeness. This book will challenge you and bless you with some laughter and deep insight into the heart of the Father and His care for us—His sheep. "And we know that God causes all things to work together for good to those who love God, to those who are called according to *His* purpose. For those whom He foreknew, He also predestined *to become* conformed to the image of His Son, so that He would be the firstborn among many brethren; and these whom He predestined, He also called; and these whom He called, He also justified; and these whom He justified, He also glorified" (Rom. 8:28-30).

Blessing as you become more like Jesus everyday!

Tom Schrock
Pastor New Community Church
Member of Board of Directors VMTC Ministry USA

PREFACE

As you peruse the table of contents, you might be saying to yourself, "Not another book on Psalm 23!" While it is true that the framework for *Becoming a Grand Champion Church* is Psalm 23, I am looking at it from a different angle and for a different purpose. The question that started the line of thought contained in this book was, how does Christ lead His church to fulfill the vision of being pure and spotless? That question brought me to the shepherding parables of John 10, which in turn opened up the duties of the shepherd as described in the twenty-third psalm. Since Christ is shepherding the church, how do the shepherding activities of the psalm apply in our local congregations? In other words, since Christ is shepherding the church, how do we participate in that work? Finding the answer to that question is the purpose and direction of *Becoming a Grand Champion Church*.

You may also look at my name and wonder, who in the world is this? I cannot provide you with a long list of academic credits. Neither can I provide credentials in the way of ordination papers. What I do offer are my years spent during my childhood raising sheep along with fifty years of growing in, worshiping in, and serving in a variety of churches. I have also spent a good number of those fifty years supporting the ministry of the church through youth leadership, Sunday school teaching, worship leading, and being an elder. I have worked closely enough with pastors to understand their hopes and frustrations while still being part of the congregation and feeling *their* hopes and frustrations. This book seeks to address the needs and hopes of both.

As you read through the book you will see that each chapter starts with a scene from my childhood when our family raised sheep to show at the county 4-H fair. My hope for these personal remembrances is to link our non-farm present with the farm-based pictures that are presented in Psalm 23. The stories are true, although some details have been fictionalized because of faded memories or for the sake of the story. For those not familiar with certain farm terms such as 4-H or "five high and a tie," I have provided a glossary at the end of the book.

Most of all, I hope that you catch the vision that Christ has for His church, where all parts function in order to lead people to maturity in Christ and ultimately present to Himself the church as a pure and spotless bride.

Dale Heinold
August 17, 2011

ACKNOWLEDGMENTS

Nothing can be accomplished without the help of others. In recognition of that truth, I thank those that have helped through various ways the creation of this work. To the reader I apologize if it comes across like so many of the other acknowledgments that you've read.

My highest praise and thanks goes to our Shepherd, Jesus Christ. I am constantly amazed at how He guides and provides for the needs of His lambs. Without His provision and guidance, this book would have been impossible.

This book would have also been impossible without my father and siblings, Duane, David, and Dianne. Thank you for allowing me to share the memories contained in these chapters. I know that reading it was not easy and stirred the grief of Mom's passing. Dad, I look back at our childhood with great fondness and respect for the love, lessons, and sacrifice that were given to us even though we did not understand them at the time. I love you all.

Two people were especially helpful during the writing of this book: Pastor Tom Schrock and Valerie Jensen. Both helped me by reviewing the chapters as they were being written. Thanks to both of you for the time, effort, and insight that you added to these pages.

Lastly, I cannot thank enough the one person without whom I could not have undertaken this project, my wife, Betty. You have endured much between my work, completing my degree and working on this project. I could not have finished this without your love, patience, and encouragement. I love you.

The Lord Is Our Shepherd

At 4:00 a.m., the alarm rudely wakes me from a sound, warm sleep. It is midwinter in central Illinois and time to check the sheep. We are in the middle of lambing season, so my brother David and I take turns making the early morning rounds to see how the expectant mothers and newborns are doing. The small flock nestled in the old barn is our 4-H project. While I am getting ready, Mom comes downstairs. Although she understands the need for this early morning ritual, she is not comfortable having one of her "lambs" leave the warm house. After putting on my parka and boots, I trudge out to the barn.

The stars shine brilliantly overhead in the clear midwinter sky. The snow squeaks with every step I take toward the weak golden light barely visible through the cracks in the barn door. A snowdrift blocks the gate, so I awkwardly climb the fence and drop into the snow-covered pasture. As I approach the barn door, I softly say, "Morning, sheep. Just me." The door protests at being disturbed but stubbornly yields to my tug. Inside the old barn, our small flock lies in deep straw. I continue my soft, one-sided conversation to calm them. One old ewe stirs and comes to greet me, hoping for a handout of some grain or fresh hay. I take my gloves off and pet her soft wool while looking over the flock. So far, Sophie has dropped triplets—normal for her—and they are doing fine. A lamb born a few nights ago to one of the yearlings is weaker than normal. We may have to help it nurse if it is going to survive. Several ewes have yet to lamb. Barney is living up to her name and is as wide as a barn; she should have twins.

There are no new lambs tonight. I throw a couple of slices of hay into the pen, knock the ice from the water pans, and return to the house for a few more hours of sleep.

Later that same day, a larger flock surrounds me. It is the gathering of the church for worship. This time I am not the shepherd, but a lamb. Others are feeding, caring, and looking over my progress. Worship, Sunday school, fellowship, evangelism, and preaching are this flock's activities. Like our barn offers our flock of sheep, the church extends its sheltering warmth from the community of believers, protecting us from the cold of the world. In one way, the purpose for our little 4-H flock and Christ's purpose for the church are the same. We raise sheep to show at the 4-H fair. Christ desires "that He might present to Himself the church in all her glory, having no spot or wrinkle or any such thing; but that she would be holy and blameless" (Eph. 5:27). Christ does this by shepherding individuals personally and through the local flock into which He gathers them.

A Different Focus

God designed sheep to be flock animals; they must be part of a flock to survive. The same is true for individual Christians. They must remain connected to a local "flock" to survive and thrive. That is why the title of this chapter is "The Lord Is Our Shepherd." This may seem at odds with the opening phrase of the twenty-third psalm, "The Lord is my Shepherd . . ." David, the psalmist, uses "my" in a way that breaks with the traditional way of viewing the shepherding role of God. The Old Testament focuses on how God shepherds Israel as a nation and how they rebel at times against that leading. So the personal shepherding of God that David describes occurs within the context of belonging to a larger flock. Christ shepherds, leads, comforts, and meets the needs for each individual through the context of the local "flock."

Many books discuss Psalm 23 and Christ's shepherding of individuals. I recommend Phillip Keller's *A Shepherd Looks at Psalm 23*. In this book, God has moved my heart to explore how Christ shepherds the local church and people, in turn, through the church. Churches become involved in so many ideas, church growth plans, and programs that it becomes easy for Christians to lose sight of what Christ is doing. My premise is simple. Jesus already has a plan and means for growing the church. He actively serves as a shepherd to each congregation. So our goal is to discover how Christ shepherds the local congregation and join Him in that work.

Declaration and Destination

The simple statement, "The Lord is our shepherd," is loaded with meaning. For the local flock, it is both a declaration and a destination. First, it is a declaration of ownership. Christ owns the flock. Jesus created each lamb and bought him or her by His own blood. "The Lord is our shepherd" is also a destination. On that journey, many temptations seek to take our focus off Him. Jesus said it best when He chastised Peter, "[F]or you are not setting your mind on God's interests, but man's" (Mark 8:33b). It is easy to "do church" in a way that pleases people but is not following the way the shepherd leads us. The Shepherd desires, though, that we follow His way and not our own.

While a local congregation may call its leader "Pastor," which literally means, "to shepherd," David declares that our shepherd is the Lord. It is important to note that David uses the name God had revealed to Moses at the burning bush: "YHWH"; I am that I am (Exod. 3:14). God says, "I am the first and I am the last, and there is no God besides me" (Isa. 44:6). Jesus also calls himself the I Am. For instance, Jesus says, "Truly, truly, I say to you, before Abraham was born, I Am" (John 8:58). Hebrews

3

13:8 summarizes the I Am, noting, "Jesus Christ is the same yesterday and today and forever." The LORD, God himself, is our shepherd.

Saying that Christ is the shepherd is not an attempt to diminish the role or need for leadership in the local congregation. It is, instead, a call to remember that no matter how the local church is structured, Christ remains the shepherd. In fact, part of Christ's shepherding the church is the provision of leadership within the flock: "And He gave some as apostles, and some as prophets, and some as evangelists, and some as pastors and teachers, for the equipping of the saints for the work of service, to the building up of the body of Christ; until we all attain to the unity of the faith, and of the knowledge of the Son of God, to a mature man, to the measure of the stature which belongs to the fullness of Christ" (Eph. 4:11-13).

Granted, people within the church disagree about the number and extent of each of these roles today. My personal view is that all the roles are still active and needed in the church. Whether you identify three of the five or all five as being active, however, does not matter in this discussion. What does matter is that Christ our shepherd provides these roles for the express purpose of growing the flock to maturity.

Three False "Gods"

Perhaps it seems obvious that Christ shepherds the local congregation. Just as clearly each congregation, like each individual, has areas where the Christ is not yet the Lord. Part of the journey is searching for and correcting those areas. While the list of possibilities is endless, I see in Scripture three areas are common to local congregations. All three cases depict idols that Israel corporately worshiped at various times in place of her true God.

The first idol is perhaps the most well known: the Golden Calf of Mt. Sinai (Exod. 32:1-8). The people become uncomfortable with Moses's long stay on the mountain and they demand that Aaron produce for them an image of God that they can worship. Out of their offerings, Aaron fashions a Golden Calf.

Whenever a congregation upholds an image of God that is incomplete or out of balance, they have forged and are worshiping a Golden Calf. For example, they can worship the God of love, but ignore justice, which is also a part of God's character. The same could also be said in reverse: idolatry can come in worshiping justice, but ignoring love. The point is that Christ is not our shepherd when we worship a vision of God that is incomplete or woefully out of balance. In these instances, we have created a god in our own image and to our own liking instead of worshiping the true God according to His revealed nature. The difficulty comes in recognizing our weakness, since we are convinced that our vision of God is correct. To defeat this idol, we must first recognize that as good as our congregation may be, it does not have all the answers. Recall what James says: "God is opposed to the proud, but gives grace to the humble" (James 4:6b).

The second idol also arises in the time when Israel is in the wilderness. Israel has sinned and God responds by sending poisonous snakes. When the people cry out for relief, God directs Moses to create a snake out of bronze and lift it up on a pole. Everyone who looks at the image receives healing from the effects of the snakebite (Num. 21:6-9). The Israelites keep that bronze snake; many years later Israel sins by worshiping it (2 Kings 18:4). This act of idolatry comes in worshiping past works of God.

It is good to recognize how God has moved a congregation along over many years. It is comforting to look back and see His hand through the trials and victories. But there is also a tendency to want to remain in the same pasture instead of following the shepherd to the next spot of green grass. There is a huge difference between knowing our history and worshiping it. Through one, we glorify God; through the other, we lose our way.

The third idol is the ephod of gold that Gideon made in Judges 8:26-27. Following the miraculous victory by Gideon's three hundred men over the Midianites, Gideon collected a tribute from the spoils. From those pieces of jewelry, Gideon formed an ephod. Scripture does not say anything about what the ephod looked like. We do know that Gideon placed it in Ophrah and that the Israelites worshiped it. One hint of what the ephod may have looked like is the description of the breastplate, also called an ephod, which the high priest wore (Exod. 28:6-21). The deep irony of the story is that Gideon's first act after his call by God was the destruction of an altar to Baal belonging to his Father. Using those clues, we see that the idolatry is the pride of being right or chosen. It is the sin of declaring that Christ is *our* shepherd but not *yours*. That something we do or teach is the right way and almost everyone else is wrong. This could be at the denominational level, local level or even the personal level. Granted, there are doctrines that must be held by all that call on the name of Christ. But in the history of the church, more division has been caused by minor squabbles then anything else. One example is the church that divided over whether a person should be immersed backwards or forwards. Our differences are not the problem; however, the pride we have in those differences is an idol and a sin.

There are of course other examples of idolatry that do not fit into those three categories. Regardless of whether the issue is one of the three mentioned or something else, when Christ reveals a problem, leadership needs to determine how to move forward to correct the sin. The good news is that Christ is shepherding His church and will provide the means of correction when the leadership and congregation are willing to follow.

The Vision

We will explore two questions through the rest of the book. The first is: how does Christ shepherd individuals through the context of the local flock? The second is: how does Christ shepherd the church? One thing is certain; Christ is patiently persistent in his shepherding. Phillip Keller notes that the twenty-third psalm could be classified as, "David's hymn of praise to divine diligence." Keller's sentiment rings true as Christ shepherds individuals to maturity and as Christ shepherds the church so "that He might present to Himself the church in all her glory, having no spot or wrinkle or any such thing; but that she would be holy and blameless" (Eph. 5:27).

A young and skinny me with a young lamb

-2-

We Have Not Lacked Anything

The hayrack quakes over the uneven ground as Uncle Howard maneuvers the train of tractor, baler and hayrack toward the first windrow of hay. The sun is high and hot. The air is scented with the pleasantly sweet aroma of drying alfalfa. Uncle Howard revs the tractor engine and engages the power takeoff which brings the baler to life. Balers are marvelously complex machines. As the tractor moves along the windrow, the hay is gently picked up, sectioned, compressed, measured, and wrapped with twine. The resulting forty-pound bale then rides up a short chute, ready to be picked up and stacked. David and I wait at the chute for the bales of hay to emerge. We are miles away from our flock. They are either enjoying the shade of the apple tree or grazing in the pasture. However, David and I have our sights on the coming winter and the need to feed our sheep until the pasture is green again. The routine of grab and stack continues until the rack is full, five high and a tie. Later in the day, these bales will be lifted into the haymow of the barn and stacked alongside bales of golden straw to wait the coming of winter.

I also recall another hot summer week. It was a few years earlier during Vacation Bible School. Along with learning crafts and songs, my age group was tasked with memorizing Psalm 23. It was hard. Each day a new verse was added, then practiced and repeated. At the closing program, our class stood and recited in unison. I did not realize it at the time, but those verses dropped

8

into the haymow of my mind, ready to be used when needed along with the other verses memorized while growing up. One other thing I recall about memorizing Psalm 23 was trying to figure out what "I shall not want" means. My young mind could not wrap itself around the poetic meaning of that simple phrase.

Needs

There is an implication that must be defined in order to understand what "I shall not want" means. It goes something like this—because the Lord is my shepherd, and He is a good shepherd, I will not lack anything that is needed. The big question that must be settled is what things are truly needed. David expands those areas of need throughout the rest of the psalm. For this chapter it is sufficient to look at the whole rather than the parts.

Who determines the needs of the flock: the sheep, the circumstances, or the shepherd? That is the question that must be answered both in our personal walk with the Lord and for the flock of Christ. Since our focus is on the flock, let's consider each in that light.

Do sheep determine their own needs? In some sense, of course, they do. Likewise there are basic needs that all humans share: the need to belong, the need for security, and the need for the essentials of food and water. But the larger question is, can the flock of Christ determine what it needs on its own? No. The appetites of the moment generally shout down wisdom and foresight. One example can be found during the wilderness wanderings of the Israelites. They grew tired of the God-provided manna and grumbled for meat such as what they had in Egypt. God heard their grumblings and gave them so much quail that it lasted for a whole month (Num. 11), or as Scripture poetically records—until it came out of their noses. This is not to infer that leadership should never listen to or seek the advice of the flock. Individuals will often rightly express their lack of some basic need but they may not understand how the Lord has planned to meet that need. For instance, the statement "I don't get anything out the sermon anymore" might be an indication that God desires to wean that person. To move them off milk and onto feed that will require effort and discipline on their part. Therefore, while the flock will be able to recognize where needs exist, they may not see how the Good Shepherd plans to satisfy those needs.

What about circumstances; can they determine what the flock needs? Of course, circumstances also play a role in determining need. However, while appetites can trip up the flock circumstances can trip up leadership. The shepherd must know the "lay of the land," where the water and the good grass are along with areas of danger. Congregations are called to minister to the needs of the community that surrounds them. So while it would be foolish to start an orphanage when there are no orphans in the perimeter of the congregation's influence, it is likewise foolhardy to jump at every opportunity that presents itself without the guidance of Christ, our Good Shepherd. However, circumstances are not always opportunities; sometimes they are catastrophes. Consider the catastrophe Moses found himself in at the Red Sea. He was leading a flock that was giddy with freedom but fickle in their desires. Moses, through God's direction, led them to the banks of the Red Sea, the army of Pharaoh threatening from behind. Sheep in this circumstance would bolt and run any way they can. But God had a plan. This conflict did not surprise Him at all. We know the rest of the story, how God provided a way of escape that also destroyed the enemy. It was a miraculous solution that did not present itself in the natural order of things. Likewise, circumstances do not catch our Good Shepherd by surprise. So while it was "foolish" for Moses to lead Israel to a place where they could be trapped, God had other plans. Likewise, perhaps it is not so foolish to build the previously mentioned orphanage because God knows the circumstance around the corner that we cannot see.

Christ, our Good Shepherd, is best at deciding what the needs of the flock are and how to meet them. Following appetite and circumstances alone will not satisfy the promise of "I shall not want." The larger picture is that Christ knows where the flock is going and growing, and He knows what it needs to get there. He knows the challenges, difficulties, and opportunities that are around each corner. He knows the needs of each member of the flock and how to best meet those needs in order to foster maturity. He knows the "foolish" things that need to be done today in order to meet the needs of tomorrow, like spending a fine summer day storing hay to provide food during the coming winter.

Seasons

My observation is that every congregation is in one of the four seasons at any given time. It is a false notion to believe that it will always be spring with new life bursting out all over the place. Spring is the time of new growth with tender shoots emerging from the warming soil and flowers bursting forth in all their glory. Summer is the time of encouragement as the young shoots mature and the flowers turn into the promise of fruit. Fall is the time of the harvest: the blade yields it matured grain and the apples sweeten to a glorious flavor. Winter is a time of cleansing, refreshment, rest from the hard work of growth, encouragement, and harvest. Many folks have a different view; equating spring with success, summer with comfort, fall with dying, and winter with dead. However, the promise of the seasons is that after winter comes spring. I have observed congregations entering into a fall/winter season; the number of people that bolted from fellowship grieved me. Their thinking was that if a congregation enters into winter, it's all over, it's dead. But that would be a false understanding and the church is weakened because of it. Winter is a time of recharging and refocusing on the Lord. It is a time for self-examination. It is a time of gathering strength for the new growth that is about to burst out when the land warms. More than anything else, it is a time of preparation for the work ahead. It is not a time of failure or a removal of the providing and protecting hand of God.

Recall Israel's winter experience as they wandered in the wilderness for forty years. God's purpose was to cleanse the congregation and to prepare them for crossing the Jordan to conquer the Promised Land. God did not remove his hand from them during their wilderness journey, but rather made it more evident. At the end of the journey Moses recorded, "For the LORD your God has blessed you in all that you have done; He has known your wanderings through this great wilderness. These forty years the LORD your God has been with you; you have not lacked a thing" (Deut. 2:7).

The Lord is our shepherd. He knows exactly what we need and when we need it. He knows which spiritual season we are in and what is coming as the seasons change. His provision may not be in accordance with our appetites or our perception of circumstance, but it will be what is needed. If we continually seek Christ and stay obedient to His direction, we will be able to say at journey's end that we have not lacked a thing.

-3-

Makes Us Lie Down in Green Pastures

I burst into the house, "Dad, something's wrong with Barney." During my normal morning chores of feeding and watering the flock, I had noticed that one of the old ewes did not come to eat. I had pushed and prodded to try to get her up but she would not budge. Dad asks a few questions and then decides to take a look for himself. In the barn, he tries to coax her up as I'd done and even puts some hay just outside of her reach. She strains her neck to try to reach it but does not try to get up.

"Strangest thing I've seen; guess we'd better call Doc Steffen," Dad decides aloud. Once we are back inside the house dad, calls the veterinarian, explains the problem, and receives the vet's promise to take a look in a couple of hours.

Every few minutes one of us glances down the hard road for Doc's blue Chevy pickup. As promised, a few hours later, he pulls in to the drive and we hurry out to greet him. Doc grabs his gear and Dad shows him to the barn. David and I walk close behind, listening to their conversation for any clue to what might be wrong. Once inside the barn, Doc looks Barney over, examines her mouth, takes her temperature, and prods her torso through the thick wool. "How soon is she due?" Doc asks.

"A couple of weeks yet, maybe three," Dad replies.

"She's got lambing paralysis," Doc said flatly. "What are you feeding them?"

"Hay and cracked corn," Dad responds.

Doc gives a little grimace, "Yep, that'll do it. Sheep need more sugar in their diet. Here's what you need to do." Doc explains how to bottle feed Barney with sugar water twice a day for the next couple of days or until she's back on her feet. He also suggests that we check with our feed man and get some sheep mix with an extra dose of molasses to add to the flock's diet. Late the next day David bursts into the house after chores and proclaims that, just as Doc promised, Barney is back up and walking around.

The Need to Ruminate

Have you ever wondered about the phrase, "He makes me lie down in green pastures" (Ps. 23:2a). It does not say that the Lord just provides plenty of good pasture but that He also makes us lie down. To understand the importance of this requires a short lesson in sheep anatomy. I will try not to make it boring. Sheep, like cattle, have a stomach with four compartments. This puts them in a class of mammals called ruminants or "those that chew the cud." While grazing, sheep do not chew their food but simply cut and swallow. Later in the day, they will sit and peacefully regurgitate to fully chew on what they have eaten. This is a necessary step to release the nutrients that are in the blades of grass that they have eaten. Providing food for the sheep, then, is really a two-step process. The first step is to lead them to the pastures with grass that is fresh and green. The second is to allow time for them to chew over what they have eaten peacefully. This is also a picture of how Christ desires to shepherd the church and those in it.

Christ's desire is for the sheep of his flock to graze upon fresh grass on a daily basis. Jesus said in the Lord's Prayer, "Give us this day our daily bread" (Matt. 6:11). When you consider other verses related to bread such as "man shall not live by bread alone, but by every word that proceeds out of the mouth of God" (Matt. 4:4) and "I Am the bread of life" (John 6:48), the full impact of "daily bread" is revealed. We as Christ followers are to seek Him on a daily basis. But, because of our church culture and the busyness of life, many in the church only eat spiritual food weekly or even less. If a shepherd only pastured the flock once a week, how healthy would it be? Sick, weak, and possibly dead. Now, before the local shepherds get offended and the sheep blame the shepherds for their condition, allow me to paint a more specific vision.

First, we must keep in mind that Christ's goal for each person is that he or she grows to spiritual maturity. One thing that separates a lamb from a mature sheep is what it eats. Lambs do not graze but drink mother's milk. In other words, the grazing and rumination of their mothers nourishes them. Essentially that is what the weekly sermon is, the result of the preacher's own feeding and meditation on the Word that is then presented in a digestible form. Whether the Word presented is easy or difficult, it is still the result of someone else's "ruminations." That is a good and necessary provision for the growth and survival of Christ's "lambs." But, milk is not sufficient for continued growth and one of three things happens. Some try to survive on a weekly intake and become weak and are easily picked off by Satan as he roams around seeking whom he can devour (1 Pet. 5:8). Some churches develop program after program to try to provide milk on a daily basis: Monday night small group, Tuesday night men's group, Wednesday mid-week service, Thursday women's group, Friday self-help group, Saturday who knows what, Sunday regular services. But, as long as a "lamb" is relying only on these things for spiritual food it will never grow to maturity. The third possible outcome is that the "lamb" becomes a disciple and relies less and less on the milk of others. This does not mean that he or she does not need the flock or a shepherd but that they can gather spiritual nourishment by reading and meditating on the Word for themself.

Growing Disciples

Why do we need disciples anyway? Would it not it be safer to simply continue to spoon-feed believers? Safer perhaps, but what happens when they enter the real world and do not know how to hear Christ? First of all, the outcome of chewing over the Word is learning to discern Christ's voice from all of the noise that surrounds us. How many folks in our churches always seem to live at the point of crisis? It is not that others do not have trouble because trouble finds us all. However, trouble becomes a crisis when we do not know how to respond or what to do next. The difference between a person who can walk through trouble spiritually unscathed and one who is always in crisis is the ability to hear the voice of the Good Shepherd through the Scriptures and apply the Word to their situation. Additionally, disciples also become leaders in various ways in the body. The number of ways that leadership is expressed is endless because of the unique way in which Christ has created each person. Lastly, Jesus commanded the church to "make disciples" as part of the Great Commission. As long as a person is feeding on milk they remain a disciple of the person providing milk; when they are able to discern the Word for themselves they become Christ's disciples and can begin to instruct others.

How do lambs make the move from milk to grazing? In shepherding, the process is called weaning. At some point, the relationship between mother and lamb must change. Typically, this is done by forced separation. However, my observation is that Christ weans each of His "lambs" in the way that is best for that individual. The change could be a slow shift or it could be very abrupt. During the process, the "lambs" may come up with some off-the-wall interpretations. Care must be taken to correct the misunderstandings while encouraging them to keep seeking. The desired outcome is that they learn to seek Christ through prayer and ruminate on the Scriptures for themselves. For the "weaned" ones, this changes the sermons and teachings of the body of Christ from milk to be swallowed to pastures that are to be grazed upon and ruminated over.

Looking back at my own life, I can see the varied ways that the Lord provided both milk and green grass for me to eat. The preacher from my earliest memory was a big man with a strong baritone voice. I do not recall a thing that he said but I do remember his big hands. The next was a young man who was destined for the mission field in Japan. I again cannot recall a specific sermon but I do remember how he strove to form relationships even though he knew that his time with us as pastor was only for a few short years. The third is the pastor of my teen years. He was a studious man who handwrote his whole sermon. From him I learned what it meant to care for the Word. The list of those who influenced me is long, of course, and includes other pastors, special speakers, missionaries, Sunday school teachers, youth group leaders, small group members, books, tapes, personal devotions, and most of all, the Word of God. Looking back helps me to appreciate my current pastor from whom I have been blessed to receive for many years. A large part of his heart and message is the desire to grow the flock to maturity.

Feed My Sheep

The Bible provides a picture of the process that we have been discussing. The scene is the restoration of Peter by Jesus after the resurrection. Three times in John 21:15-17, Jesus questions Peter's love and three times gives him a specific instruction concerning care for the flock. "So when they had finished breakfast, Jesus said to Simon Peter, 'Simon, son of John, do you love Me more than these?' He said to Him, 'Yes, Lord; You know that I love You.' He said to him, 'Tend My lambs.' He said to him again a second time, 'Simon, son of John, do you love Me?' He said to Him, 'Yes, Lord; You know that I love You.' He said to him, 'Shepherd My sheep.' He said to him the third time, 'Simon, son of John, do you love Me?' Peter was grieved because He said to him the third time, 'Do you love Me?' And he said to Him, 'Lord, You know all things; You know that I love You.' Jesus said to him, 'Tend My sheep'" (John 21:15-17). Jesus' instruction to Peter is to "tend [feed] my lambs," "shepherd my sheep," and "tend [feed] my sheep." Notice the progression in both the maturity and the activity. Tending to lambs is different than tending to mature sheep. The role of local leadership in feeding the flock is identified in these three directives. "Tend my lambs"—make sure they are getting the milk that they need for growth. "Shepherd my sheep"—lead the "lambs" to maturity and discipleship by providing the guidance, discipline, and love of a shepherd. "Tend my sheep"—lead the mature to the green grass and encourage them to ruminate upon the Word of Christ. Through these three activities, the shepherd provides the appropriate spiritual nutrition for the spiritual maturity of the individual. The result is both growth in maturity and an increased reach into the world.

-4-

Quiet Waters

"Hold her still" David yells, his hands gently cradling a young lamb.

"I'm trying," I retort, my arms tightening around the bucking yearling's neck. We had noticed that the new mother was not tolerating the nursing of her lamb. The new sensation made her skittish; this meant that the lamb was not getting enough to eat. Dad suggested that we help her to get over her fear. The plan is simple: a couple of times a day for the next few days force her to hold still long enough for the lamb to nurse properly. Unfortunately, the yearling is not one of last year's show sheep so she is not hand tame.

Sheep, being flight animals, are easily spooked by anything new. A new noise, a new experience, even a new sheep can upset them. But, they can also become accustomed to these new sensations. We spend several weeks each summer getting show sheep used to being led by the hand, poked and prodded by the judge, and subjected to the noise of a crowd. All of that work is necessary so that when it comes time to lead them into the show ring they will stand still.

Finally, I get the yearling to quiet. David places the lamb near the udder and encourages her to eat. As the young lamb bucks up against the udder the yearling tenses. "Easy girl," I whisper. David grabs a bit of hay and offers it to the young mother. We both watch the lamb feed, her tail twitching excitedly as she drinks the mother's milk. After a few minutes, the lamb wanders away and lies down. I release the yearling. She bolts at first but returns to a slow walk after a few steps and heads straight for her lamb. They nuzzle for a few seconds until the yearling is convinced that we did not harm her baby.

After two days, it only takes one of us to help the lamb nurse. It is stronger and the mother is calmer. After four days, we don't need to help at all; the yearling is now used to the new sensations.

It is amazing how the atmosphere around our congregational gatherings can rapidly turn from peaceful to troubled. I recall one time when I was visiting a church with some family. The worship time was fantastic and there was the contented feeling of family in the air. The pastor got up to make a few announcements. The final one changed everything—he announced his resignation. It was obvious that only a few in the congregation knew what was coming. It was as if a wave had ridden over us, turning joy to anxiety. Even though we moved on with the service there was an undercurrent that even I, as a visitor, could feel as quiet waters quickly turned to troubled waters.

Quiet Waters

How does, "He leads me beside quiet waters" express Christ's shepherding of the church? The sheep do not find quiet waters by accident; the shepherd must lead them to it. Since we have already touched on Christ's leadership in previous chapters, we will concentrate on "quiet waters."

In my mind, "quiet waters" is a picture of the atmosphere that must be present when the congregation, the flock of Christ, is gathered. When turmoil reigns, when the "waters" are troubled, there is no rest for the flock and they cannot drink deeply from the water of life. However, in church life it is not the outward appearance that must be peaceful, as some suppose, but what is happening in the spiritual realm. I have visited congregations that maintained an outward peacefulness: the music was soft, people spoke in whispers if at all, and children sat quietly or were busy elsewhere. But, just beneath the calm surface was tension and unforgiveness; relationships were strained and turmoil reigned. I have also been in noisy venues that on the surface appeared to be in turmoil but held a deep feeling of peace and family. This observation does not indicate that all quiet congregations are in turmoil or all noisy congregations are peaceful. Instead, it is an observation that the atmosphere of a congregation cannot be judged by what is external but rather by the depth of love that they have for each other and for the Lord.

The world is full of trouble and turmoil. The gathering of the flock should be one place where those seas are calmed. In Revelation, John gives a vision of what is in Christ's mind for the church. "Then he showed me a river of the water of life, clear as crystal, coming from the throne of God and of the Lamb, in the middle of its street. On either side of the river was the tree of life, bearing twelve kinds of fruit, yielding its fruit every month; and the leaves of the tree were for the healing of the nations. There will no longer be any curse; and the throne of God and of the Lamb will be in it, and His bond-servants will serve Him; they will see His face, and His name will be on their foreheads. And there will no longer be any night; and they will not have need of the light of a lamp nor the light of the sun, because the Lord God will illumine them; and they will reign forever and ever" (Rev. 22:1-5). In this text, we see water as clear as crystal, calm, and undisturbed; the tree of life bearing fruit all year round, the leaves of which are healing for the nations. The sacrificed yet living lamb, Jesus Christ, sits on the throne. His bondservants see His face, are sealed with His name, and are always illuminated by His presence. Yes, this is a picture of the coming kingdom in its fullness and it is also a picture of Christ's desire today as His church gathers.

Troubled Waters

It is against Christ's vision for the church that war is waged. Two of the primary weapons are confusion and distraction. The wielders of these weapons are the forces of darkness in the heavenly places (Eph. 6:12). Their purpose is to trouble the waters of the congregation so that the sweet water of the Holy Spirit is polluted with bitterness (James 3:11).

Confusion is the first weapon. The apostle Paul cautioned the Corinthian church about it, "For God is not a God of confusion but of peace, as in all the churches of the saints" (1 Cor. 14:33). It is interesting that one definition of the Greek word translated "confusion" indicates rebellion: as one lexicon puts it, "to rise up in open defiance of authority." This works well with the context of Corinthians as people rose to prophesy in a way that disrupted the flow of the service. The range of the weapon of confusion runs from simple misunderstandings to outright rebellion. Confusion can be caused by simple things such as the worship slides being out of order. The more damaging strikes are those that are rooted in rebellion. Unforgiveness, perfectionism, people-pleasing, and partiality are all examples of confusion-generating rebellion. Perhaps that list surprised you a bit. Think about it for a second. If I have unforgiveness, I am being rebellious against the command of Christ to forgive my brother and to love him as I love myself. This generates confusion because my life is at odds with the scriptural mandate. Perfectionism is rebellion because it expects others to be perfect while being blind to my own sin. People-pleasing is rebellion because my actions are determined by fear of what others may say or do and not the rule of Christ. Partiality is rebellion because it elevates or debases a person based on external standards instead of how Christ sees them. Essentially, confusion and rebellion are any things that unseat Christ from the throne and replace Him with idolatry and pride.

The second weapon in the enemy's arsenal is distraction. I do not think that there has ever been a gathering of believers where distractions have not occurred. Can you imagine dealing with the distraction of a young man falling out of a third-story window and dying? Paul did in Acts 20:9-12. After praying for the young man and restoring his life, the service continued until daybreak. It is simply impossible to remove all forms of distraction from our gatherings. Why? Because the problem is not the cause of distraction but allowing ourselves to be distracted is. Granted, there must be a desire to minimize distraction where possible. But a total elimination of distractions is impossible.

Leadership can employ two strategies to deal with distractions. The first is to ignore them by continuing with the activity of the moment as if the distraction did not exist. The second is to embrace the distraction, which opens up two doors. The first door changes the distraction into a teachable moment, as Jesus did with the children in Mark. "And they were bringing children to Him so that He might touch them; but the disciples rebuked them. But when Jesus saw this, He was indignant and said to them, 'Permit the children to come to Me; do not hinder them; for the kingdom of God belongs to such as these. Truly I say to you, whoever does not receive the kingdom of God like a child will not enter it at all.' And He took them in His arms and began blessing them, laying His hands on them" (Mark 10:13-16). The second door allows those in the congregation to categorize the distraction and deal with it so that they can mentally refocus on the Lord as the service moves on. For instance, a young mother decides not to take her newborn to the nursery. During the sermon, the child begins to cry. Embarrassed, the young mother gathers her things and takes the child out. It would be a simple thing to say, "Praise God for new life!" This would ease the mother's embarrassment and let the congregation categorize the event and put it aside.

It would seem that distractions just happen, which they do, but the enemy also uses them to draw away attention at critical points. Distractions seem to strike most often when our spirits are ready to receive the Word of God in a life changing way.

Our defense against the devil's scheme is laid out in James, "Submit therefore to God. Resist the devil and he will flee from you" (James 4:7). The Lord is our shepherd that leads us to quiet waters. Submission to Him means staying focused on His guidance and not on the surrounding circumstances. We are to be aware of circumstances but not focused on them. James says to "resist the devil"; Paul writes in Ephesians to stand firm. When confusion, rebellion, and distraction happen, they must be resisted with a firm stance so that our focus remains on Christ. This applies to our lives in addition to our gatherings.

When we are gathered together discernment is needed to determine what avenue the enemy is using to poison the atmosphere. Is it bitterness? Disappointment? Distraction? Rebellion? Confusion? Untimely words? Unforgiveness? Judgmentalism? Pride? Anger? Woundedness? Apathy? Discouragement? The list could go on and on but the battle plan is the same: submit to God and resist the devil. Take discouragement, for example. Submitting to God means to grasp fully that Christ is shepherding the church and that the congregation must choose to follow Him and leave the results to Jesus. Resisting the devil's weapon of discouragement means to stop judging achievements as a means of discerning Christ's leading; it is like driving down the highway by only looking in the rearview mirror. As we stand firm in our resistance to the enemy's schemes the promise of Christ is that he will flee, the waters will calm, and the flock will be refreshed because the Good Shepherd led them there.

A lamb feeding

-5-

He Restores Our Soul

It's a warm summer day and the whole family is in the barnyard. David and Dad are getting ready to lift one of the lambs that will be shown at the fair. I am standing by at the front of the sheep stand; my job is to buckle a leather strap around the lamb's neck to secure it to the stand. Although there are fancy stands, ours is fairly simple. It's a short platform made up of 2x4s and painted white. At the front, where I'm standing, is another 2x4 that rises up from the platform; the top is slightly curved and the remains of one of Dad's old leather belts is nailed to the top. The purpose for this seeming instrument of torture is to hold the lamb still while we wash and trim its wool. On one side of me is Dianne, our little sister. Mom is standing on the other side, her arms loaded with towels and a bottle of Ivory dish soap.

"Ok Dave, on three: one, two, three—lift." As they lift the lamb, I guide its head onto the post and quickly get the belt around its neck. When Dad and Dave release their hold, the lamb tries to get away and almost falls off the stand. Dad reaches under the stand and retrieves the kinked garden hose. He gently wets the lamb's wool with the cool well water. When he is satisfied that it is wet enough he kinks the hose again and places it under the stand. Mom squirts a few lines of Ivory soap on the top and sides of the lamb. I lift Dianne so she can stand next to the lamb's head and we all begin to rub in the soap. Our hands are busy moving the soapsuds all over the lamb's body; no part is left out. When Dad is satisfied, he grabs the hose and begins to rinse out the suds. The lamb's transformation is marvelous. When we had put the lamb on the stand, it's wool had been a dingy grey. It is not that the wool looked dirty, but it was as if grey had been its natural color. After the washing, the wool had changed to a beautiful white; not the cool, bright white of snow but a warmer white, more like an eggshell.

While Mom and Dave towel off the lamb, Dad hands me the Sheffield Shears and says, "Here, trim off the dingleberries." My look of curiosity asks the unspoken question, "Huh?" He leads me to the rear of the lamb and points to the half dozen or so blackberry size balls of hardened manure that are attached to the lamb's wool. Equipped with my new word, *dingleberry*, I gently pull each one away from the lamb's body and remove it with a quick clip. Once Dad is satisfied that the lamb is clean, we release it from the stand and lead it into the barn to a special stall with a deep bed of clean straw.

Although there are many church experiences that have been restorative in my life, the most dramatic one outside of salvation came through a little known ministry called Victorious Ministries Through Christ. The centerpiece of their work is a prayer ministry session. Think of it as a one-on-one time with God where, with the help of at least two prayer ministers, sin is confessed, the stain of the world is removed, and the dingleberries of Satan are cut away. The soap used is the blood of Jesus that is applied through confession, repentance, renunciation, and forgiveness. To be honest, it feels a little scary going in—somewhat like when you go to the dentist or doctor. But coming out there is a joyous feeling that is difficult to fully describe. The closest I can come is the feeling of being revived, like stepping out of a cool shower after a long, hard, hot, sweaty day.

Restoration

Restoration can apply to several different things, such as having health returned after an illness, having strength returned after a rest, or having something returned to one that has been stolen or lost. In general, it is the return of something back to its original condition. All of these are contained within, "He restores my soul," and the Parable of the Lost Sheep. The parable is part of a series Jesus told concerning the finding of lost things. The religious folks were giving Jesus a hard time about hanging around sinners, the outcasts of their society. Luke records it this way, "So He told them this parable, saying, 'What man among you, if he has a hundred sheep and has lost one of them, does not leave the ninety-nine in the open pasture and go after the one which is lost until he finds it? When he has found it, he lays it on his shoulders, rejoicing. And when he comes home, he calls together his friends and his neighbors, saying to them, 'Rejoice with me, for I have found my sheep which was lost!' I tell you that in the same way, there will be more joy in heaven over one sinner who repents than over ninety-nine righteous persons who need no repentance'" (Luke 15:3-7). This parable shows us that Christ searches diligently for each stray lamb and rejoices when it is found. Joy and rejoicing are key words in these verses and strike at the center of self-righteousness. A person or church that is self-righteously religious does not respond with joy but expects punishment; some form of retribution for the wrongs committed. But when Christ found each of us He did not say, "what took you so long?" Instead, He and all of heaven rejoiced. Since the attitude of Christ our Shepherd is joy when a sinner repents, it must be ours as well—not just the first time, but also every time.

Focusing in again on our primary question, how does the church join into Christ's shepherding work of restoration? Seek, wash, trim, present. Seek diligently those that are lost. Wash with the blood of Jesus. Cut off the residue of the enemy. Present each lamb under our charge to the Good Shepherd at the end of the age.

Seek Diligently

The church is not built to be a ball field in Iowa: "If you build it they will come." The first step of Christ's restoration of sinners is not the born-again event but the seeking that precedes it. Each expression of the flock of Christ needs to be about the business of finding the lost. Part of this is helping and teaching folks to be willing seekers and showing them how to seek. Another part is providing opportunities through special events. The point is that one aspect of Christ's shepherding is seeking actively and diligently for the lost. This means braving the world to find them and not just opening the doors hoping they wander in. From my experience, this is the part that most Christians and most churches have the hardest time with but at which, if asked, they think they are doing just fine. *Diligently* is the key word. The shepherd in the parable did not go out for an hour and try again a few months later. He kept at it until the lost sheep was found. We don't know if that took hours or days but he kept at it. Also, he did not hire a professional finder; he searched for the lamb himself. No one is exempt from seeking. Seeking is not to be left up to the evangelist. Nor is the pastor the only one from a congregation that is to seek. Seeking the lost is everyone's responsibility. You see, Christ is the one seeking and He has tasked all of us with helping.

Wash Thoroughly

Getting clean begins but doesn't end with new birth. Isaiah writes, "'Come now, and let us reason together,' Says the LORD, 'though your sins are as scarlet, they will be as white as snow; though they are red like crimson, they will be like wool'" (Isa. 1:18). The cleansing agent is the blood of Jesus shed on the cross. There is nothing else in the world that can remove the stain of sin. Have you ever tried to "un-dye" a piece of cloth? It is impossible. A hint of the dyed-in color will always be there.

But what is impossible with man is possible with God. His declaration is that He can perfectly remove the sin stain. That is a work of restoration and re-creation. But God does not restore us back to our pre-sin state, nor to Adam's pre-fall state. Instead, He restores and re-creates us in the image of Christ (Rom. 8:29, 2 Cor. 3:18). From practical observation, it is obvious that while the transference from the kingdom of darkness to the kingdom of light is instantaneous, the work of transformation is continual. The implication for the flock of Christ is that there is a necessary first washing of conversion but also continual washings though confession and repentance as Christ restores, reforms, reshapes, and re-creates each person's character.

Cut Off the Residue of the Enemy

The third aspect of the shepherd's restoring of our soul is the removal of bondages to the flesh, the world, and the devil. These bondages act like puppet strings that seek to pull us off the path of righteousness. They are the results and consequences of our own sin and possibly the sins of others. They can affect our thinking, our emotional responses, our imagination, and our choices. Sometimes they are simply bad habits that need to be crucified. But often there is a demonic component that needs to be cut off in order to be free. Too often, the church washes thoroughly but does not seek to heal the consequences of sin to the soul. James speaks about the double-minded man in James 1:8 and 4:8. He tells us that a double-minded person is tossed about by everything that comes along. In the later chapter he says, "Submit therefore to God. Resist the devil and he will flee from you. Draw near to God and He will draw near to you. Cleanse your hands, you sinners; and purify your hearts, you double-minded" (James 4:7-8). It is important be cut free from the bondages of our past sin, cut free from the puppet strings that seek to pull us from the path of righteousness, and remove the dingleberries that seek to condemn us even though we've been washed clean by the blood of Christ.

The purpose for all of this activity is the eventual judgment of our works for God's kingdom. The Bible in 1 Corinthians 3:12-15 speaks of a judgment of fire that tests everyone's work in the kingdom. "Now if any man builds on the foundation with gold, silver, precious stones, wood, hay, straw, each man's work will become evident; for the day will show it because it is to be revealed with fire, and the fire itself will test the quality of each man's work. If any man's work which he has built on it remains, he will receive a reward. If any man's work is burned up, he will suffer loss; but he himself will be saved, yet so as through fire." The Bible also speaks of crowns given as rewards. However, I think that all of us would be exceedingly blessed just to hear Jesus say, "Well done my good and faithful servant." Our desire must be to hear those words spoken not only to us, but also to those for whom we have responsibility, and those alongside whom we labor in the kingdom of God.

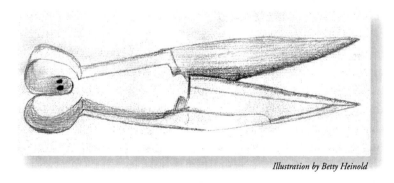

Illustration by Betty Heinold

Sheffield Shears

He Guides Us in the Paths of Righteousness

All the work of the previous month was for the next few moments. "Now in the ring, Hampshire lamb class; next up in the lamb class, Shropshire," rang the announcement from the loudspeaker. I hop over the short fence and into the square pen that holds my lamb. I place one hand underneath the lamb's jaw and begin to pick off the straw that clings to its wool. The lamb by now is used to this and stands still with just the lightest touch. I nod at Mom and she opens the gate so I can lead the lamb out. Two pens down, Dad is doing the same for David. We both lead our lambs out of the show barn to a place just outside of the entrance to the show ring. Mom, Dad and Dianne help us give each lamb a once over for cleanliness. In the background, the loudspeaker crackles as the judge awards the ribbons for the Hampshire class and briefly explains his reasoning. A few moments later, the Hampshires leave the ring and walk by us. "In the ring now . . . Shropshire lamb class; next up Suffolk." David and I, along with two others, lead our lambs, each with the same crouching walk with one hand under the lamb's jaw and the other on the lamb's tail. We position ourselves in a line abreast and plant one knee in the ring's sawdust; the other is positioned in front of the lamb's breast just in case it bolts. The judge gives us a few moments to set up and position each lamb's feet. The crowd is softly talking. Mom, Dad and Dianne have moved to the stands alongside our grandparents. I recognize many of the faces: neighbors, friends, and other folks from the surrounding areas. The judge approaches our lineup (continued in the next chapter).

Paths

While there is but one gate to righteousness, there are many paths on the other side. In other words, we are challenged to walk out our righteousness in every pathway, relationship, experience, challenge, opportunity, and pain in life. Christ shepherds His flock by leading us along these paths. Every path also has two components, the final destination, and the features of the path at that moment.

Up in the mountains in the Copper Canyon region of Mexico is the small village of Maguarichi. The only way there is a narrow winding dirt road through the rugged hills and valleys of the region. Sometimes the road dashes through streams. Other times it hangs precariously along the walls of the canyon, a steep face on one side, and an even steeper drop on the other. Now imagine driving a big white van full of high school aged kids on a mission trip up that narrow road. Each one handled it differently, some thrilled at the sights, others were bored, and a few got sick. But, we all made it.

Take, for instance, the path of righteousness called marriage. There are points along that path where the going is easy; the road is broad and the scenery beautiful. But harrowing moments also occur when the path is narrow and must be followed with care. The destination is the fulfillment of the vows to love, honor and cherish through it all until we are separated by death. The same thing could be said of the other paths of our children, relationships, occupations, and service. All of these paths intertwine and move toward the destination of appearance before God in Zion. "How blessed is the man whose strength is in you, in whose heart are the highways to Zion! Passing through the valley of Baca they make it a spring; the early rain also covers it with blessings. They go from strength to strength, every one of them appears before God in Zion" (Ps. 84:5-7). The point is that our walk with God is not static. It is not a one-time experience that simply spins us in a new direction. Instead, it is an intentional, every moment of every day walk where we choose with each step who we will serve. At any point along the path we should be able to look back and join Fanny Crosby in singing, "All of the way my Savior leads me; what have I to ask beside!"

Righteousness

The definition of righteousness should be familiar: right standing with God not of our own making but through the blood of Jesus; yes, amen. On to the next topic, we have this down—or do we? Even in the law, God had two purposes for righteousness: a right standing with Him and right living with each other. "He has told you, O man, what is good; And what does the LORD require of you but to do justice, to love kindness, And to walk humbly with your God?" (Mic. 6:8). So while we are righteous through the blood of Jesus we are also tasked with living that same righteousness through our lives.

The question that we need to ask ourselves is, "What is the righteous requirement for the moment that I'm in right now?" This is where the fruit of the Spirit comes in. We are capable neither of saving ourselves nor of dealing with each of life's moments in the full righteousness of Christ through our own strength. We need the fruit of His love, His joy, His peace, His patience, His kindness, His goodness, His faithfulness, His gentleness, and His self-control for each moment, each choice, and each reaction of life.

The paradigm, our understanding, of righteousness needs to change from being something we possess to something we are. That was what Jesus challenged the Pharisees about. They put on a cloak of righteousness; they acted righteous but were not righteous. Jesus did not mince any words with them. He told them plainly, "So you, too, outwardly appear righteous to men, but inwardly you are full of hypocrisy and lawlessness" (Matt. 23:28). Jesus' words also remind us that righteousness does not work from the outside in but from the inside out. We don't need to act righteous; we need to be righteous. It is something that should come out of us automatically as a part of our fiber and being. When something happens and we react poorly instead of responding righteously, the next question we ask ourselves is vital. If we ask, "What can I do differently next time?"—then we are asking the wrong question. The right questions are "Where does my heart need to change?", "What sin is hiding there?", and "Where is the dark corner that bred this reaction?" As Jesus said, "Make sure that the light you think you have is not actually darkness. If you are filled with light, with no dark corners, then your whole life will be radiant, as though a floodlight were filling you with light" (Luke 11:35-36, NLT).

Guide

Returning to our central theme, since Christ is guiding the flock, how do we join Him in this activity? How do we participate in leading others in righteousness? While the sermon or the Sunday school lesson may have aspects of guidance, they are not the sole or most important places where the activity of guiding occurs. The same can be said of counseling and prayer since they too are part but not the whole. We guide by allowing others to follow our walk. This is not just true of the identified leadership but of anyone who may be seen as an example. How the janitor reacts when the tile is scuffed with black marks is guiding. How a fellow parishioner corrects the child of another that is misbehaving is guiding. How a leader deals with the challenges in his or her personal life is guiding.

On that last point, allow me to speak something to the people. Stop expecting your leadership to act perfectly at all times and in all situations. They will not do so and neither will you. The Bible is full of stories that contain both the triumphs and the failures of leadership. Moses, even after being so enveloped by presence of God that his face glowed, needed the advice of his father-in-law. Also recorded is when Moses reacted out of anger at the people's complaint and struck the rock contrary to God's direction. David, a man after God's heart, committed deceit, adultery, and murder. Paul got into a church fight with Peter and Barnabas and yet wrote most of the New Testament. Yes, we need to deal with the moral failures of persons in leadership. But we also need to give them the grace to be real instead of making them into marble statues that, although perfect, are lifeless.

Our Guide

We cannot leave this discussion without emphasizing that it is Jesus who is guiding us in the paths of righteousness. There are many folks trying to convince us that the path lies over there, or that something that we believe is not righteous. In the final analysis, they are nothing more than the false christs that Jesus warned us about. "And then if anyone says to you, 'Behold, here is the Christ'; or, 'Behold, He is there'; do not believe him; for false Christs and false prophets will arise, and will show signs and wonders, in order to lead astray, if possible, the elect" (Mark 13:21-22). The Scriptures are our signposts along the path and clearly mark which way to walk. But it seems that some folks desire to change the signposts. We must not fall into the trap of bending the Scriptures to the values of our society and age. If we do, the result is that we are no longer following Jesus' guidance but our own desires and have stopped walking in the paths of righteousness.

Jesus' desire is that we follow him in the paths of righteousness but he also warned that the path would require sacrifice. He told us clearly us that "If anyone wishes to come after Me, he must deny himself, and take up his cross and follow Me. For whoever wishes to save his life will lose it; but whoever loses his life for My sake will find it" (Matt. 16:24-25). This requirement is the same for churches as it is for individuals. The local church is blessed as it maintains the vision of following Christ no matter what may come. Our watchword must be "where Jesus goes we will follow."

Left to Right, myself, David, and Dianne
in the show ring

For His Name's Sake

The judge slowly circles our lineup of lambs. Beginning with the first one in line, he checks their teeth, runs his hand down their spines, and feels the muscling at the shoulders and haunches. The last lamb in line jumps at the touch of the judge but the boy is able to hold on. My lamb tenses at the disturbance. The judge then places himself in front of the line. He points first to David. David moves his lamb forward and takes up a new position indicated by the judge. The grin on his face is enormous. Next, the judge points at me. I maneuver my lamb next to David, catch his eye, and give a congratulatory nod. While I'm repositioning my lamb the judge indicates the positions of the final two. The loudspeaker squeals a bit as the volume is turned up. The judge then talks through why we are finishing in this order. The deciding difference between David and I are the breed markings on the sheep's faces. This judge prefers a more open face with less wool. The 4-H Fair Queen then walks down the line handing each of us a ribbon: David and I both receive a blue ribbon, and the other two both receive red. There is also a white ribbon but none was given out for our class. I take my ribbon and hang it from the lamb's ear; it twitches at the unusual sensation. We then guide our lambs back out and to the pens where Dad, Mom, and Dianne wait to help put the lambs away and begin to get the Ewe class sheep ready. Above our pens are white signs that indicate our names and that of our 4-H club, the Prairie Livewires. Taking the ribbon from the lamb, I tack it to the sign for all to see.

One of the things that I thought was strange growing up was when the pastor would say something like, "and now to continue our worship service," when transitioning from song to preaching. At that age, I saw worship as the singing since that was when we were focusing on God. The preaching, although good, seemed to be directed at us, which to my mind did not seem to be worship. It wasn't until much later that I was able to broaden my perspective of worship to include all that we do for the Lord.

Why Do We Do?

Why do we do what we do when it comes to church or anything else that connects Christianity with real life? That is a very challenging question. Isaiah 26:8 says, "Indeed, while following the way of Your judgments, O LORD, We have waited for You eagerly; Your name, even Your memory, is the desire of our souls." The NIV translates it as, "Yes, LORD, walking in the way of your laws, we wait for you; your name and renown are the desire of our hearts." This verse is easy to agree with but difficult to walk out. It challenges us to desire to exalt Christ's name, His renown, and His reputation as the motives for our actions.

Whose name is more important in our church, Jesus', the pastor's, or the name on the sign in the yard? It is pretty easy to proclaim Jesus as the center of our worship service. But, what about everything else that makes up church life? Is Jesus' name and renown the desire of our hearts at the business meeting? When we do the work of an evangelist, are we seeking to build up our church or seeking to add worshipers to the kingdom? The list, of course, could go on and on.

The attitude of seeking Christ's glory should be ever increasing in our lives. Each person grows through an arc, from being the receivers to being the givers; an arc from where church is about them and what they can get out of the service to it being where they seek to glorify Jesus in everything. The transition is not easy, automatic, or simple. It is at the tipping point, when the balance is shifting from self-centered to Jesus-centered, that many trip and fall. Some leave one flock seeking to "be fed" when Christ is instead calling them to feed others. Some turn this to an extreme and leave the church altogether, declaring that the church is itself self-centered because it wants to use their gifts, talents, and abilities without compensation or acknowledgement. Through this wrong-headed attitude the enemy of our souls twists the very purpose of being "living stones" in order to destroy the church. Paul in Ephesians describes what each believer should grow into. "As a result, we are no longer to be children, tossed here and there by waves and carried about by every wind of doctrine, by the trickery of men, by craftiness in deceitful scheming; but speaking the truth in love, we are to grow up in all aspects into Him who is the head, even Christ, from whom the whole body, being fitted and held together by what every joint supplies, according to the proper working of each individual part, causes the growth of the body for the building up of itself in love" (Eph. 4:14-16). In this verse, Paul is describing a vision of the church built up in love that glorifies our Lord. That kind of love is the fulfillment of Isaiah 26:8 that we read earlier.

A Question for Leaders

To leaders, by the evidence of your position, you should have completed the arc from receiver to giver. The questions then change along with the places where one may stumble. If we were sitting face to face and I asked you, "To whom or what does your church belong?" I have no doubt that you would appropriately reply that the church belongs to Jesus Christ. However, knowing the right answer and living the answer is the difference between religion and faith. The point where this can be practically examined is when leadership must make a decision. Let me propose a hypothetical situation that I believe can be more broadly applied. Suppose a teen leader approaches leadership with the desire to take the youth on a mission trip to Mexico. He presents a well laid out plan and there is no practical reason to refuse. There are four possible responses, only one of which is truly seeking after the "name and renown" of the Lord. The first is to agree without much consideration; this is probably the hardest to weigh because it could indicate either a large degree of trust in the teen leader or a cop-out to shift responsibility. The second is to respond out of pride. The consideration is not what would glorify the Lord but how uplifting would be the effect on the church's or personal reputation. Of course, this could flow the other way as well, with a rejection that seeks to protect the reputation of the church or leadership. The third is to decide based on the pleasure or anger of others. People-pleasing changes the focus from the spiritual to the political. It may be expedient for the moment but in the end leads to an accumulation of wood, hay, and stubble that when tested with fire will be burned away. The final choice, of course, is to make a decision based on what would glorify Jesus. Leadership must rely on the guidance of the Holy Spirit to find the answers to not only the monumental decisions that face the flock but also the everyday decisions.

Worship Leaders

Allow me to take a short side trip and speak directly to worship leaders. I have been on the worship team or leading worship for over thirty years. The same traps of pride and people-pleasing that were mentioned above can also affect your ministry. Be aware of these traps and avoid them in yourself and in your team. Choose the team carefully. I have found that for my team I would rather have a humble but less-talented individual than a prideful individual with impeccable talent. Why is that? I believe the enemy desires worship leaders and their teams to fall into the same sin that he did, taking the glory of God and claiming it for themselves. Of course, this could happen to anyone who serves or ministers, but it seems especially prevalent in worship ministry.

Humbleness goes beyond the worship time; it must also be present in the relationship between leadership and the worship team. It is imperative that worship ministry operates in submission to the leadership of the local flock, whether or not there is agreement with all of their decisions; whether or not you have worked for hours perfecting a certain song that gets put aside at the last minute. We must trust what God is doing and how He is directing the flow of the service through the leadership.

One last encouragement for worship leaders and team: Remember who your audience is. In a normal concert, the audience consists of those sitting in the seats. In our worship services, the audience is the Lord. In essence, we are not singing and playing to entertain one another but we are leading a choir of praise and worship that includes all present. Yes, there is a second edge to the worship time that seeks to bring us together in unity and to encourage faith but the primary purpose is praising God. In the end it does not matter how tight the harmony, how exact the rhythm, or how perfect the pitch. What does matter is that people have been invited into the throne room to praise and worship the Lord.

The Judgment

So, the day has finally come and we are standing in front of the judgment seat of Christ. There is a promise and exhortation given to leadership in First Peter, "Therefore, I exhort the elders among you . . . shepherd the flock of God among you, exercising oversight not under compulsion, but voluntarily, according to the will of God; and not for sordid gain, but with eagerness; nor yet as lording it over those allotted to your charge, but proving to be examples to the flock. And when the Chief Shepherd appears, you will receive the unfading crown of glory" (1 Pet. 5:1-4). Paul speaks about standing before the throne and presenting those that have been in his charge, "We proclaim Him, admonishing every man and teaching every man with all wisdom, so that we may present every man complete in Christ" (Col. 1:28). The judgment will concern why we did what we did. Did we glorify Christ or ourselves? Did we follow our own way or the leading of the Holy Spirit? Did we mature the flock or simply entertain it? However, this judgment is not limited to leadership. Our lives are to glorify Christ. This is not a church thing; it is a life thing. We are to glorify Christ in all things. "Whatever you do in word or deed, do all in the name of the Lord Jesus, giving thanks through Him to God the Father" (Col. 3:17).

Walking Through the Valley of the Shadow of Death

February 1973

The alarm releases an incessant buzz, time for the 4:00 a.m. check. I sleepily put on my clothes and make my way downstairs toward the kitchen. Mom quietly emerges from her bedroom and follows me downstairs. In a ritual that we repeat throughout the cold of lambing season, she sits at the kitchen table while I put on my parka and boots. Neither of us says anything; her presence alone repeats the previous expressions of care. Even though a thaw has wiped away the snow and the temperatures have warmed, my heart fears what I may find in the barn. This winter we have lost several lambs through a variety of things, some were lost to the cold, others were not able to compete with larger siblings, and some fell to unknown illness or birth defect. As I open the barn door, the familiar sights and smells speak of warmth and comfort. As usual some of the old ewes rouse and come looking for a handout of fresh hay that I willingly provide. After knocking the ice out of the water and refilling the pan, I search for the lamb that I am worried about. She lies over in a dark corner. To an uninformed observer she simply looks weak, but I know she is dying. In young lambs, the telltale sign is the ears: they will stand erect until close to the end when they droop as if to say that there is not even enough energy left for this simple activity. Tonight her ears are drooping for the first time since we first noticed her stumbling about. I gently pet the lamb; tears run down my cheeks as I try against hope to bottle-feed her. Although she takes some of the milk, as she has done before, it does not seem to have any positive effect. I know that later today she will be dead. I slowly plod back to the house. As I enter the kitchen, Mom sees my tears. "What's wrong son?" She asks.

"We're going to lose another lamb, its ears are drooping," I reply while wiping my tears and trying to put on a brave face.

"You've got a tender heart, son, never lose that," she said, getting up from her seat. "You've done all you can, now it's up to God." Her arms gave me a quick hug and we both went back to bed.

Late November 2010

I push a button on my cell phone while driving to work. "Call Dave," I order the voice dial. After the obligatory confirmation, it starts to ring. Dave answers with his customary lazy "hello." We talk for a few moments about where he is trucking to today. I change the conversation to the reason for the call: "Remember how the lambs' ears drooped before they died?"

"Yeah," he replied.

"Mom's leaning last night reminded me of that. I think that we are down to days instead of weeks."

"I saw that the night before too. It's not a good sign," he replied.

"It's going to be hard on Dad, not to mention Grandpa and Grandma. Are you going to be home tonight to help Dad get her to bed?"

"Not with this weather. It's going to be slow going with the snow."

"Ok, I'll run down and help tonight. I'm pulling into work so I gotta run. Drive safe."

"Yep, let me know how things are going. Bye."

"Bye."

Within two weeks, Mom went home to Jesus. She died at her home. Present at her side were her husband of fifty years, all three of her children, two of our spouses and one grandchild. Her death was peaceful. The peace of that moment lasted through our prayer as we held hands around her bed. Following the "amen" and a few tearful hugs, we began the flurry of notifying hospice, family, pastors, and friends. My wife and I walked down the short block to where her parents lived to inform them. We were all at the deepest point of the valley of the shadow of death.

Our journey had begun before we even knew it. In late July, Mom had begun to have problems with her eyes and balance. At a family campfire in mid-September, she could not walk at all but enjoyed the gathering until the coyotes started to howl. Dad reported later that she had had a very anxious drive home that night. We had also noticed that her dream world was intruding on reality; she was convinced that she made a trip to St. Louis to visit my son and his pregnant wife. It was a trip she was never able to make. In October, while Betty and I were away at a VMTC school, we got a late-night call from Dad. Mom had Creutzfeldt-Jakob disease. CJD is a prion disease for which there is no treatment or cure and that is always fatal (see appendix). Its effects are similar to other forms of mental degeneration although the timeline is tremendously compressed. It was hard receiving that news away from home, but the believers at the school made up for being away from home and family.

While our family's descent into the valley of the shadow was gradual, that is not always the case. Just a few days prior to Mom's passing, one of her friends unexpectedly died of a heart attack in the early morning. One of the points of humor at Mom's funeral was the imagined meeting in heaven between MaryAnn and Mom. We could just imagine Mom's surprise and her saying something like, "When did you get here?" While we had been slowly walking into that valley since her illness began, MaryAnn's family was thrown into it over the cliff. This is important to recognize because there are no uniform experiences concerning the valley of the shadow. There is no predicting its depth, darkness, entrance, or exit.

The Church and Loss

Those unknowns make it hard for the church to deal with loss. There is a timeline surrounding death, its arrangements, and the funeral that the church handles excellently. The expressions of care are manifold; gifts of food, help with housekeeping, cards, memorials, flowers, and friends just being there are all a comfort. During the times that follow, however, there seems to be a lack of knowing what to do. The time between the funeral and the eventual walking out of the valley is the loneliest. You see, the church family has dealt with their grief and they are ready to move on; the valley is shallow for them.

That does not mean that reality is ignored. One problem, however, is that the question, "How are you doing?" is generally expressed at an inappropriate place and time when it is uncomfortable to fully respond. Another problem is that the typical first answer of, "Okay," or, "As good as can be expected," is seldom followed up. It is a huge social catch-22. We have to ask the question to feel that we have expressed care but are generally glad that it does not go much deeper because we are ill prepared to deal with it. At the same time, the person being asked may be tired of the question and at one level is glad not to be probed further. But it must be recognized that the answer, while being socially acceptable, is patently short of the truth. In addition, our society does not deal well with grief, desiring instead to bury it quickly. Adding it up, we are simply not equipped to receive or give this ministry of comfort.

Based on my own weakness in this area, my own experience, and my own observations of others' grief, I offer these suggestions to church leadership:

- Recognize that all grief is unique to the moment. A person may respond differently to loss based on any number of variables.
- Encourage the immediate expressions of comfort but also recognize that the valley does not end one week from the funeral but possibly many years after the loss.
- Do not take the word of the aggrieved as final when they respond to caring questioning by saying they don't need anything. They may not know what they need. They may be embarrassed to ask. They may be too proud or too humble to ask.
- Ask probing questions at times and places conducive to them being answered truthfully and heard fully. Many folks will not delve into personal feelings in the presence of others.
- Train other leaders how to care for loss. This is not a condemnation because most do not come by this ministry naturally. For example, one of the leaders in our body confessed to me that he did not know how to respond or what to say to me after Mom's death. I've been there myself and understand his feelings of being inadequate for the moment.
- Understand that although loss through death is the deepest form of the valley of the shadow, there are other losses that also take people through the valley. Any loss could qualify, such as the loss of a job, going through divorce, the death of a pet, or the loss of something hoped for. These are often overlooked but can be the training ground for the deeper valleys.

Jesus Knows the Pain

In this area, Jesus is also shepherding His church. Part of the shepherding is through the Gospel proclamation of Christ's victory over death. Another is realizing that Jesus also experienced the pain of separation from his Father on the cross when he cried, "My God, My God, why have you forsaken me." Because of the work of the cross, we no longer need to suffer eternal separation from God. So Christ's work in the valley is two-fold: the comfort in the knowledge that Christ has already removed the sting of death and His empathizing comfort to ease the pain of separation that comes with death and loss.

During my time in the valley, one phone call meant a lot to me. One night a Christian brother, who had experienced the loss of his father a few years prior, called to ask how I was. He did not take "fine" for an answer. Instead, he briefly related some of his own past feelings. His empathy and his own past pain opened the door for me to share my own feelings in a deeper way than I had with anyone else. I refuse to call it a simple thing because it is not. This kind of comfort requires time, openness, and the courage to push through the shells of protection. It is a difficult yet exceedingly necessary ministry.

I will leave leadership and congregation with this encouragement: We often gravitate toward the enjoyable ministries. There is no greater joy than leading a sinner to repentance or seeing an old scar healed. However, there are also ministries that are difficult and poke at our own past or future pain. Ministering grace to those walking through the valley of the shadow of death is one of those difficult ministries. It is, however, a necessary ministry and one that needs to be strengthened in our congregations.

-9-

Fear no Evil

This particular story occurs during the first year that we kept sheep. The barn is occupied with Uncle Howard's pigs so our sheep have taken up residence in the apple orchard with its rustic, and much smaller, chicken house.

We are all in the living room watching Red Skelton. Dad is sitting in his recliner with his feet up. Mom is on the davenport, knitting needles clicking as she works on some project. The three of us kids are lying on the floor enjoying the antics of the show. The phone in the kitchen rings. "Dale, run and see who that is," Mom says. Reluctant, I hop up and run to the kitchen because a Freddy the Freeloader sketch is just starting. "Hello?" Over the connection, I hear the voice of our neighbor.

"Hey, this is Ron, we just got home and there are some sheep down at the corner—I think they might be yours."

"Thanks, we'll check." Worries begin to assault me. Did I shut the gate? What if a car kills one? How is Dad going to react? I hurry back to the living room and announce, "Ron thinks our sheep are out." Dad flips the lever on the recliner, Mom puts her knitting down, Dave starts to get up, and Dianne keeps watching Freddy. There is a flurry of action as Dad locates a couple of flashlights, Mom picks up Dianne and we all rush out to the pasture. To my relief the gate is securely latched. Dad shines his flashlight toward the orchard and does a quick headcount. It is quick because we only have three sheep to begin with and we can see only one in the beam of the light. "Judy," Dad orders, "take Bluebell and the boys. See if you can find them. I'll see if I can find where they got out, I'll bet they broke through that old wire fence in the back." We hurry over to the blue Plymouth and pile in. Mom gets it started and pushes the R button, backs around, pushes the D button and points the car down the lane to the hard road. "Ron said they were at the corner," I inform as we near the end of the lane. Mom turns left onto the blacktop and says, "I hope that they don't get in the corn, we'll never find them." The turn in the hard road comes into the beams of the headlights and just as Ron said, both of the wayward ewes are in the ditch grazing on the long grass. David and I hop out, neither of us quite sure what to do. Our experiences with moving sheep have always been in tightly controlled situations. Now, we try to herd them but they just peel off to the side and run further away. We try to catch them, but even when we do manage to grab some wool, we cannot hold on. They just don't cooperate. Eventually David does tackle one and manages to get it under control. The next worry is how to get it back. Mom suggests that we load it into the back seat of the Plymouth. This is a new experience for the ewe and for us but we manage to get her loaded. Mom hands me a flashlight. "Keep an eye on the other one, we'll be back." As she turns the car around I can see David sitting in the back with the ewe and Dianne standing on the front seat reaching back and petting her head. While they are gone, I try to get close to the remaining ewe but she is having none of that. So I stand and wait for the Plymouth to return. It seems to be taking long time to unload and come back. I wonder if they are having trouble or if the sheep messed in the back seat. How's Dad coming with the fence? How are we going to catch this one? Eventually I see Bluebell's headlights heading down the lane and turning my way. When she comes to a stop, Dad and Dave step out. "Being stubborn?" Dad asks. I explain what I've tried and that I can't even get close. Dad opens the back door of the car and pulls out a near-empty feed sack. "Let's try this trick," he says and rattles the bag while softly calling "here sheep." The ewe raises her head up at the sound of the grain tumbling about in the bag. She comes closer hoping for a handout. Dad reaches out and tries to grab the ewe but she quickly backs off. He laughs and says, "We'll have to do it the hard way." So with Dad driving and David keeping a flashlight on me, I walk along the road coaxing the ewe forward with the feed sack until we eventually get her back home.

We Fear No Evil for You are With Us

King David's declaration is said in the context of man's greatest fear, death. But the implication of this Scripture along with many others is that Christ is with us in the midst of this fear and all others. Another Psalm declares, "The LORD is my light and my salvation; whom shall I fear? The LORD is the defense of my life; whom shall I dread?" (Ps. 27:1). Paul extends this sentiment further in Romans 8:33-39. He begins by asking, "Who will bring a charge against God's elect?" and further amplifies it a few lines down with, "Who will separate us from the love of Christ?" He then lists things that, although evil in their own right, are not strong enough to divorce us from Christ's love. They include tribulation, distress, persecution, famine, nakedness (extreme poverty), peril, and sword. A few verses later he continues the list but also includes some things not evil: death, life, angels, principalities (meaning things demonic), things present, things to come, powers, height, depth, or any other created thing. Nothing, nada, zip, zero can separate us "from the love of God, which is in Christ Jesus our Lord!"

Just because none of these things can separate us from Christ's love does not remove their existence in our lives. The world still mocks, Satan still assails the church, and people still become offended. Those are the practicalities of the Christian life. Reading through church history, it's a wonder and a miracle that she still exists at all. Through the intense persecutions of the early years, the political intrigues and power plays that vexed the church after Constantine, the interfaith persecutions that occurred in the wake of the reformation and the strong divisions that followed, to the scandal ridden, apathetic church of today, it is a wonder. But through it all, the Holy Spirit shepherded the church. We of this generation receive the blessing of the many that have preceded us and we are called to extend those blessings into the coming generations no matter how the world, Satan, or mankind's folly tries to hinder.

Fear

A necessary step is to understand what we fear. From what I have observed and experienced, fear can be broken down into three sources: fear of loss, fear of pain, and fear of rejection. (There is, of course, some obvious overlap such as the emotional pain that is sometimes caused by rejection.) These fears strike both individuals and congregations. However, fear in itself is not evil. It can either spur us on towards greater works of faith or keep us from them. What often makes the difference is how we respond to the threat or challenge that is causing fear.

Risk consultants identify three ways to respond to any threat or challenge. The first is to accept the risk. This is seen in the story of Daniel and the Lion's Den. He knew about the law that threatened death to anyone that prayed to any deity other than the king. Daniel chose to accept the consequences and prayed to God, as was his practice. Accepting the risk is a heads up decision that knows the risks but moves ahead anyway. The second is risk mitigation. This means to move ahead but take measures to limit the risk or the damage. To some degree, this is seen in Moses at the burning bush. When God told him to free the Children of Israel, he feared that they would reject him. God mitigated that risk by instructing Moses to say that "I Am" sent him. Mitigating the risk is also moving toward the risk but protections are employed to soften or deflect possible harm. The third is risk avoidance. One would think that since the Bible is a book of faith that there would not be any examples of risk avoidance;

however, that would be wrong. Take for example Paul fleeing the city of Damascus at night by being lowered over the city walls in a basket (Acts 9:22-25). Risk avoidance is seeing danger and moving in the opposite direction. All of these can be the right thing to do and the wrong thing to do.

Wisdom

How do we know which of the three risk responses is the right path? Wisdom. But, here we must be careful, for there are two types of wisdom. James identifies these as natural wisdom and godly wisdom. He describes natural wisdom as being earthly, natural, and demonic. It operates from jealousy, selfish ambition, and pride, and results in disorder and every evil thing. Natural wisdom can be sourced in experience, "common sense," societal pressures, or demonic influence. Godly wisdom's source is "from above" or from God Himself. It operates from humility, love, and faith, and results in holiness (purity), peace, mercy, and good fruits. James also describes it as "unwavering without hypocrisy" (James 3:13-18). Godly wisdom is acquired by asking in faith, "But if any of you lacks wisdom, let him ask of God, who gives to all generously and without reproach, and it will be given to him. But he must ask in faith without any doubting, for the one who doubts is like the surf of the sea, driven and tossed by the wind. For that man ought not to expect that he will receive anything from the Lord, being a double-minded man, unstable in all his ways" (James 1:5-8). And it begins with the fear of the Lord, "The fear of the LORD is the beginning of knowledge; Fools despise wisdom and instruction" (Prov. 1:7). And, "The fear of the LORD is the beginning of wisdom, And the knowledge of the Holy One is understanding" (Prov. 9:10). The fear of the Lord is a little-understood phrase because it flies in the face of our understanding that God is love (1 John 4:8). There is a terrifying aspect of being in God's presence as seen in the throne room scene of Isaiah and John's experience at encountering the glorified

Christ in Revelation (Isa. 6:5, Rev. 1:17). However, the place where wisdom and the fear of the Lord intersect is authority. To fear the Lord is to count His authority in our lives and church as being above everyone and everything else. God's authority is the source or beginning of wisdom.

Observations

So how are these insights applied to our search for how Christ is shepherding the church? The first observation is that in the midst of a fearful situation, Christ is leading; He is there in the midst of it with us. Another observation is that we must do our part by seeking His wisdom through prayer. Ideally, this should start long before the situation arrives or is even on the horizon. The third observation is the recognition that God's guidance does not always "make sense." It is often not the prudent thing to do nor does it always follow the path of least resistance. Notice that Psalm 23 does not simply say, "do not fear." It says that even when going through the valley of the shadow of death, a place of great fear, I shall not fear *because* Christ is with me. Christ the shepherd is guiding us through the valley. Relying on natural human wisdom and common sense will get us stuck in the valley; following godly wisdom will lead to bright sunshine and green pastures.

Your Rod and Staff Comforts

A barn swallow buzzes my head, flies through the open barn door, slices around two pillars and then darts back outside through an open window. Some birds sing, some look pretty, but barn swallows are God's stunt pilots. Even though it's mid-summer, all of the sheep are penned in the barn so we can dose them with de-worming medicine. As Dad explained it, they pick up little worms that live on the grasses that they eat which can then live on in their digestive tract.

"Do you care which one first?" David asks.

"Nope," I respond while handing three boxes of pills to Dianne. Dave climbs over the gate, grabs an old slow-moving ewe, and walks her over to the gate. "Give me two pills, sis." She plucks two of the large white tablets from the Styrofoam tray. I take them from her hand. Two barn swallows quickly circle, unsure if they want to fly by but then dart through the door. I load the pills into the end of the plastic tube; it is about six inches long and has a plunger to push the pills out. The business end of the tube is scarred where the sheep have gnawed on it over the years. I nod at Dave. He tightens his grip on the ewe. I lift her head back and work open her jaw. I run the tube into her mouth trying to get far enough back so that she has to swallow the pills. She tries to reject the tube gnawing at it and pushing against it with her tongue. I push the plunger, yank out the tube, and let go of her head. Did she swallow or is she chewing? Looks like this one swallowed. I open the gate a little; Dave shoves the ewe through the opening. He then turns to capture the next victim. A barn swallow dives out of nowhere, darts through one window, draws a circuit around the sheep, and dances back out through another window.

The Shepherd's Rod and Staff

The word "rod" in Psalm 23:4 has a two-fold meaning. The first is as a tool of discipline. In Proverbs, the primary focus of discipline is fools and children: "A whip is for the horse, a bridle for the donkey, And a rod for the back of fools" (Prov. 26:3). "Foolishness is bound up in the heart of a child; the rod of discipline will remove it far from him" (Prov. 22:15). However, Scripture also indicates that God disciplines all of his children. "For those whom the Lord loves He disciplines, And He scourges every son whom He receives" (Heb. 12:6). God's discipline is rarely fun but there is joy in the end as we see that another aspect of ourselves has been molded into the image of Christ. The second meaning of rod is that of authority or governance. For instance, in the blessing given by Jacob to Judah in Genesis 49:10, we read, "The scepter shall not depart from Judah, nor the ruler's staff from between his feet, until Shiloh comes, and to him shall be the obedience of the peoples." The NASB uses the term scepter but it is the same Hebrew word found in Psalm 23:4. To hold the rod is to hold authority.

The word "staff" has the simple meaning of something to lean on. I liken it to an old-fashioned hiking stave, which is basically a straight stick that is used to help provide balance over difficult terrain. For instance, say that you are crossing a small stream and the stepping-stones are unstable and unevenly spaced. Planting the staff in the stream before each step makes it easier to cross over safely. The staff also provides a means of support: if there is no high ground or rock from which to watch over the sheep, the shepherd must stand. In order to ease that burden the shepherd leans on the staff.

Comfort

So how do these add up to the psalmist's view of providing comfort? Why didn't David write about a warm blanket and a cozy fire for his metaphor? They are much more comforting than a rod and staff. How then do we make sense of what David is saying? Things just do not seem to add up. There is, however, a missing part of the equation, which is found in the heart of the shepherd and the desires of the sheep.

The heart of the shepherd is to protect the health of the sheep so that they can grow physically and in numbers. In other words, when the shepherd employs the rod and staff it is always for the good of the sheep. Using the rod to punish a wayward lamb that likes to wander off is for its own protection because safety is found in the flock. The ruling aspect of the rod is seen in the leadership of the shepherd as he chooses with great care where to take the flock, what pastures to graze on, what ponds to drink from, and when to retreat to the confines of the sheepfold. The shepherd leans on his staff so he can better watch for predators and if needs be uses it as a weapon against them.

The desires of the sheep are also part of the equation. When a lamb is rebellious, always seeking its own path to greener grass, it is in dangerous territory; not because the grass is not good but because it moves outside of the protection of the flock and the shepherd. For it, discipline does not bring comfort. However, the lamb that desires the safety of the flock does find comfort when it wanders away and is brought back by the rod. Since the desire of the sheep is for good food and water, they are comforted by the shepherd's guidance, knowing and trusting that the shepherd will lead them to good places. The flock's desire is also to stay safe from predators and they are comforted by seeing the constant vigilance demonstrated by the shepherd standing among them leaning on his staff.

Pastoral Role

It is perhaps easy to see how Christ is shepherding his flock in Psalm 23:4 with what we just considered. We understand that Jesus cares for us, disciplines us when we need it, leads us where we need to go, and is ever watchful over the flock. How then does the local flock join to this aspect of Christ's shepherding?

You may have noticed that in previous chapters I used the generic term "leadership" instead of pastor, reverend, priest, elder, or bishop. The reason is that these terms are often misapplied and therefore cause confusion. It is common in the evangelical world to call the lead minister Pastor even when that person's primary gifting and operation is something else such as teaching or evangelism. We have turned a role into a title. And with it we have added innumerable expectations of what pastors are to spend time doing. But God did not construct His flock to work like that. Instead, He expects all of the flock to contribute their gifts and talents to the working of the flock. Some will be encouragers, some will exude empathy, others will teach, some will see to physical needs, some will excel at seeking the lost, others will see other opportunities; the list is infinitely long. However, discipline should be at the hand of the pastor or under pastoral authority; the flock is not designed to be self-policing. In my experience, self-appointed policemen or "watchmen" (Ezek. 33:6-7) almost always do more harm than good. What I mean by "self-appointed" are those that have not been given that role by leadership even if they believe Ezekiel 33 is their appointment from God. Leadership or governance should rest in the hands of the pastor, especially in matters concerning works of the kingdom. I know that statement is contrary to the congregational political model. However, if the pastor is to shepherd the flock, which is the literal meaning of the word, they must be empowered to lead and direct the congregation according to God's wisdom.

The pastor is to be constantly surveying the flock, watching for danger and predators. Even when the flock is content, he is watching for the enemy. He also watches for strays and seeks to bring them back in so that all stay within the safety zone of the flock. But pastors must not do any of this on their own strength. The flock must see them leaning on the staff of their personal relationship with Christ. This then balances the need to lead authoritatively with the humbleness of relying on Jesus. Leaning on the staff of Jesus also keeps two things in perspective. The first is that Jesus is the shepherd of the flock and the pastor or leader is assisting in that work. The second is that ministry to the flock is all about the needs of the flock and not the personal gain of the shepherd. By personal gain, I do not only mean money but also the emotional gains of feeling important that many seek. It is not wrong for the flock to see to the physical needs of leadership but that must not be the focus of the shepherd. Instead, the shepherd is to focus on what is best for those under their care.

There is in Ezekiel a negative example of the shepherd's role. In it, God is prophesying through Ezekiel about the failings of Israel's leaders and priests. As you read it watch for the improper use of the rod and staff.

> Then the word of the LORD came to me saying, "Son of man, prophesy against the shepherds of Israel. Prophesy and say to those shepherds, thus says the Lord GOD, woe, shepherds of Israel who have been feeding themselves! Should not the shepherds feed the flock? You eat the fat and clothe yourselves with the wool, you slaughter the fat sheep without feeding the flock. Those who are sickly you have not strengthened, the diseased you have not healed, the broken you have not bound up, the scattered you have not brought back, nor have you sought for the lost; but with force and with severity you have dominated them. They were scattered for lack of a shepherd, and they became food for every beast of the field and were scattered. My flock wandered through all the mountains and on every high hill; My flock was scattered over all the

surface of the earth, and there was no one to search or seek for them." (Ezek. 34:1-6)

Compare now Jesus' mission statement as He quoted from Isaiah, "The Spirit of the Lord is upon Me, because He anointed Me to preach the gospel to the poor. He has sent Me to proclaim release to the captives, And recovery of sight to the blind, to set free those who are oppressed, to proclaim the favorable year of the Lord" (Luke 4:18-19). When pastoral leadership properly exercises the rod and staff in step with Jesus there is a blessing for the flock. Of supreme importance to God is the attitude and motive of the shepherd. The motive of local leadership should be the good of the flock as expressed in the Word of God. This means seeing to their spiritual growth, nourishment, and safety. It also means bringing discipline at times for the good of the flock.

The flock of Christ then must realize that what they think is best is not always what the shepherd sees as best. Our sheep did not like having deworming pills shoved down their throats but it was for their health and growth. On the other hand, they loved the soft grass, fresh water, sweet hay, and tasty grain that we provided for them. This, then, is the comfort of the rod and staff, knowing that Jesus and local leadership are seeking the good of the flock and not their own comfort.

You Prepare a Table Before Me In the Presence of My Enemies

I watch as the 4-H judge circles the three contestants and their ewes in the show ring. Having graduated from high school, my showing days are over. Dianne is currently in the ring, halter leading a Cheviot ewe she calls Babe. Cheviots are the smallest of the show breeds but are harder to handle since they tend to be skittish. Training and practice though has paid off and Babe contentedly stands next to Dianne's wool skirt. The judge must be in a hurry since he skips the normal hands-on examination and heads to the microphone. "Frankly, I don't like this breed since it serves no purpose, being both too small and short-fleeced. While each presenter has done very well handling their ewes, the ribbons that I've chosen reflect the value of the breed. The ewe in first place receives a red ribbon . . ." At first there is a shocked silence in the crowd, followed by angry and confused chatter. Dianne, in first place, receives her ribbon with grace from the 4-H queen but is near tears.

"That stupid judge," Dad spits out as we make our way to the show barn. "I've never seen a judge refuse to give out any blues. I just don't understand it." Dianne exits the ring with Babe following peacefully on the lead. Mom gives Sis a hug, releasing her tears. David takes Babe's lead and leads her back to the pen. One of the show organizers comes over and pulls Dad aside.

"I'm sorry about that, Duane. That judge had no right to do that but there's not much I can do. And I hate to tell you this but even though your daughter placed first she can't show for Grand Champion; only blue ribbon winners can be in the ring. All I can tell you is that he won't judge here at Eureka ever again if I have any say." Dad nods and silently walks away while thinking through what the organizer said.

Several weeks later, the reason for the judge's confusing call became evident at the Future Farmers of America (FFA) show. This is a larger show since it covers our county and three or four others. Many of the same competitors from our county's 4-H fair are here.

Dianne hand leads Babe into the ring and lines up with four other competitors. Because there is no style competition, she is wearing blue jeans, a white blouse, and her blue FFA jacket. The judge performs his examination. He places Dianne in first place and awards her a blue ribbon. After a few more classes have passed through the ring, it is time for the Grand Champion competition.

Dianne again brings Babe to the ring. David follows with his ewe since he won the Shropshire class. Several faces in the ring are familiar from our 4-H show including the Suffolk entry that won this year's Grand Champion. The question for the judge is, of the various breeds represented, which one is the best example of its particular breed against the other breeds presented. The judge circles slowly, carefully examining each entry. It seems that one of two breeds, either the Suffolk or the Hampshire, always wins. Both are big meaty sheep and favored in the industry. Shropshires are a little bit of everything breed while Cheviots have been bred for hardiness over size and fleece. The judge approaches the microphone. "This was a difficult choice. Each breed is well represented. However, the Grand Champion is the Cheviot shown by the young woman."

The Banquet

The fifth verse of Psalm 23 marks a shift in metaphors from shepherding to that of a royal banquet. It is easy to visualize this as a reference to the marriage supper of the Lamb alluded to in Revelation 19:9. That feast will be a time of celebration where those that belong to Christ are the guests and the Father is the host and preparer of the feast. A few years ago, I played host in some sense to such a banquet at our daughter's wedding reception. While it wasn't the most lavish of celebrations it was still a type of what the psalmist had in mind. The event was by invitation only. We all ate and celebrated the beginnings of a new family. As the father of the bride, I was grateful and pleased to spend the money needed for the celebration. Can you imagine the wedding feast God has planned with his infinite budget?

If David had stopped with "you prepare a table for me," all would be understandable and good. But he added "in the presence of my enemies." What does that mean? From what I have found there seems to be an Old Testament view and a New Testament view that, although seemingly contradictory, are actually complementary and still active in the church today.

The Old Testament view can be seen in Isaiah 25. In the opening verses, it praises God for destroying a city while protecting the weak. "For You have been a defense for the helpless, a defense for the needy in his distress, a refuge from the storm, a shade from the heat; For the breath of the ruthless is like a rain storm against a wall" (Isa. 25:4). Isaiah then shifts to a future look at the banquet that God will prepare. "The LORD of hosts will prepare a lavish banquet for all peoples on this mountain; a banquet of aged wine, choice pieces with marrow, and refined, aged wine" (Isa. 25:6). Verses 10-12 speak of the future humbling of Moab through being "trodden down" and having his pride laid low. Preparing a banquet in the presence of our enemies envisions victory for God's people while our enemies must stand and watch but not participate in the feast. Think of Samson's last act. Blind and humbled, he is led into a feast of the Philistines to be entertainment through his humiliation. God, of course, had the last laugh as Samson brought the house down.

The New Testament view exemplified by Jesus is seemingly contradictory. There are several examples: Jesus eating with the tax collectors and sinners that, while not His enemies, were not exactly on His side either. Or, another banquet where Jesus was the honored guest of a Pharisee but was not treated like one until a prostitute came in and washed His feet with her tears. But perhaps the most poignant is the Last Supper where Jesus established Communion as both a remembrance of His sacrifice and a foreshadowing of the marriage supper. This He did in the presence of His enemy, the friend that would betray Him. Jesus modeled that instead of humiliating the people that wage war against us, we are to win them over.

Real Enemies

That does not mean that enemies as a concept has been stripped from the New Testament. Instead, the spotlight has shifted to the real enemies. The first is the demonic realm, "For our struggle is not against flesh and blood, but against the rulers, against the powers, against the world forces of this darkness, against the spiritual forces of wickedness in the heavenly places" (Eph. 6:12). Other enemies are the false philosophies and speculations of the world, "We are destroying speculations and every lofty thing raised up against the knowledge of God, and we are taking every thought captive to the obedience of Christ" (2 Cor. 10:5). The final enemy is sin, "In your struggle against sin you have not yet resisted to the point of shedding your blood" (Heb. 12:4, ESV). Our enemies are the satanic realm, the worldly philosophies that war against the truth, and our own sin. Concerning the men and women through whom these attacks come, Jesus said, "You have heard that it was said, 'You shall love your neighbor and hate your enemy.' "But I say to you, love your enemies and pray for those who persecute you, so that you may be sons of your Father who is in heaven; for He causes His sun to rise on the evil and the good, and sends rain on the righteous and the unrighteous" (Matt. 5:43-45). To relate this to modern warfare: Our battle is not with the front line troops, the men and women through whom the attack comes, but on the supply lines along with the command and control structures that empower them.

Winning the Battle

How then does Christ lead His flock in this battle? While there are several strategies, there are innumerous tactics employed to fight the good fight. Let me state first that our goal is to capture the front line troops, to bring them over not as imprisoned enemy combatants but as brothers and sisters in Christ. To that end, then, there are the artillery of prayer, the sword of the Word of God, and courageous humility.

Prayer is the most powerful, most misused, and least understood activity in the church. Too often, it is simply the thing to do at this point in the meeting. But prayer can change things, often things that we cannot see and may never know. A woman in our church prayed for her father's salvation for thirty years. Eventually those drips of prayer eroded his hardened heart and he committed his life to Christ. To be honest, prayer is a huge subject of which many good books have been written. Perhaps the most important correction that I see is that prayer needs to change from being focused on our needs to being relational with the Father. I have some family that only calls when their computer is broken because they know I can fix it. They are using our conversation to fix a need in their lives but there is no relationship, there is no communication outside of that narrow band. To be frank, it is very annoying. I can imagine how God feels when all that His children do is offer prayers that contain more petition than conversation. Recall that it was the relationship factor that drove Jesus' own prayer life. Why is relational prayer important?—because it shifts our focus from our needs to the Father's desire for the situation. As we learn the Father's heart, our prayers become guided missiles that will destroy the works of the enemy.

The second strategic weapon is the Word of God, and like prayer, much as been written about the Word. Let me give this one encouragement. Read the Word for what it says, not for what we think or want it to say. God's Word is more powerful when we take it out of the scabbard of our pet doctrines and let it slice through the enemy with unhindered power. We do not need to explain it but we do need to release it to speak for itself. For instance, how often do we hang around certain favorite verses that speak to our personal conviction but ignore others that challenge our understanding? Church leaders especially need to be honest brokers of the Word, letting it speak instead of using it to prop up their own speculations. The unleashed and unfettered Word will tear down speculations, separate soul from spirit, and divide truth from error.

The final strategic weapon is courageous humility. At first, this may appear to be an oxymoron but that is because we have a false conception of humility as being weak and fearful. James says to submit to God and resist the devil (James 4:7). Above all else, humility is submitting our will, thoughts, plans, ambitions, and desires to the will, thoughts, plans, ambitions, and desires of God. Humility does not mean lowering ourselves before other men as much as coming under God. But this does not open the door to being arrogant or boastful before others because, as 1 Corinthians 13 says, love is not those things. Courage is both standing firm against the tide of the enemy's attacks and moving forward according to God's will, thoughts, plans, ambitions, and desires. Bring the two together and you have a picture of Jesus that we are to emulate.

God's preparing a table before us in the presence of our enemies, then, contains the two-fold meaning of success in bringing sons and daughters of darkness in to the light of Christ in order to join us in the feast, and success in realizing victory over the enemies. It is not our power, strength, and ability that make things happen, it is the power and grace of a loving God.

Dianne in the show ring with a Cheviot ewe

-12-

You Have Anointed My Head With Oil

The summer sun is hot and bright overhead. The ewes and lambs are temporarily locked in the barn. They are not exactly sure what is going on but are enjoying the grain that we used to lure them in. After giving them a few minutes to enjoy the meal, we begin to separate the lambs from the ewes. The ewes are pushed back out to pasture while the lambs are moved to a separate pen. The lambs have grown nicely since their mid-February births. They are no longer as frisky, they rarely jump about on all four legs, and they have long since graduated off mother's milk.

Shortly after their births, we had marked the lambs with copper rings in their ears. The number and placement of the rings vary depending on the owner and mother of the lamb. Eventually they outgrow the small rings and need to have them replaced with permanent tags.

Dad stands by with the notebook containing the marking record and a box with strings of green, red, and blue plastic ear tags. Each color signifies the owner, David's are green, Dianne's are blue, and mine are red. They look like squished ovals; one end has a small gap that widens when you pull the sides apart. On one side of the tag, HEINOLD is stamped in white letters; on the other is a number, also in white.

While Dad stands outside of the pen, David and I begin the process of catching the lambs one by one. David wraps his arms around the neck of one. While he holds it still, I check the copper rings. "This one has one on the upper left middle and two on the left bottom inside," I report. While I clip off the copper rings, Dad checks the notebook.

"That is one of David's," he replies. He pulls a green tag out of the box, looks at the number, and records it in the notebook. I take the ear punch from my back pocket. The placement of the hole is important; there must be enough room for growth but it cannot be too dangly or it will catch and tear off. Taking careful aim, I squeeze the hole punch. The lamb jerks but David has a firm hold. Dad hands me the tag. I spread it a little and work it through the oval hole until the closed end of the tag is secure in the hole. Dad opens the gate enough to let the lamb through; it runs off twitching its right ear as if to get rid of a pesky fly.

The Anointing

The anointing spoken of in the twenty-third psalm is not the anointing of kingship that we see recorded in the story of King David. Neither is it the anointing of the priesthood or prophet, nor the anointing of the coming Messiah. It is the anointing of fellowship.

As we have seen in the previous chapter, the context for this line in verse 5 is that of a banquet. As the guests arrive, servants wash their feet and pour fragrant oil on their heads. We learn of this tradition, which is far different from our own, in Luke 7:36-50. Jesus is attending a meal at the invitation of Simon, a Pharisee. At some point during the meal, a prostitute comes in and begins to anoint Jesus' feet from a vial of costly perfume. The Pharisee becomes silently indignant. Jesus, knowing the man's thoughts, challenges him with a parable on love and forgiveness. During Jesus' response, we learn that Simon did not perform the customary welcome. Jesus said to Simon, "you did not anoint my head with oil, but she anointed my feet with perfume." In this age of daily baths and Old Spice, we may have a hard time understanding the reason for pouring oil on someone's head when we have them over to eat. While we could guess about body odor and the general dustiness of the environment, it is enough to notice that it was a customary part of hospitality.

While the anointing of the king denotes authority to lead; the anointing of the priest, authority to intercede; and the anointing of the prophet, authority to speak, this anointing is not about power or authority. The anointing of fellowship is a mark of acceptance and family. It speaks of welcome, friendship, and belonging. Perhaps you have had the experience of meeting a Christian brother or sister for the first time and yet after a few moments feel like you have known them for years. That is the effect of the anointing of fellowship and being part of the family of God.

Does this mean that we need to start pouring oil on guests as they arrive at our home or church? The means of expressing friendship and acceptance varies from culture to culture and even from church to church. In North America, the wave expresses the bare minimum level of welcome, a handshake is often the norm, and a healthy hug is, perhaps, the maximum. But people of other cultures, such as many Europeans, may greet one another with kisses on the cheeks. Regardless of the method, be it anointing with oil, a handshake, hug, or a chaste kiss, the meaning is the same: that of welcoming each other and accepting one another's presence.

Welcoming Hospitality

It is perhaps obvious how this applies to the local church. How we greet each other and visitors is important. Our expressions of welcome and acceptance are a vital activity of the body that is easily overlooked. For leadership, the pressures of responsibility and preparation can place welcoming the flock and each other low on the task list. In addition, in American culture we are becoming more disconnected from each other even while maintaining a veneer of communication. The more technology replaces face-to-face or even voice-to-voice communication, the more disconnected people become. This creates a dual problem: people long for fellowship yet are losing the ability and skills to connect outside of their "virtual world." This is one reason that I am suggesting we elevate the welcoming of each other from its relatively low position to a higher place. Call it teaching through modeling or getting the ball rolling, but unless the church discovers the value of a simple welcome, we risk losing the platform to touch people. But before the flock assumes that welcoming is all on the shoulders of leadership, let me clearly say that it is not. Welcoming is part of hospitality and fellowship which belongs to every part of the body.

The welcome is, however, just the first step. When considering the local body, the remainder is all about hospitality and family; in other words, fellowship. Fellowship is not simply the occasional meals that we participate in as a body. Fellowship happens whenever the flock is gathered. It contains our interactions with each other and is another way, in addition to worship and preaching, the Holy Spirit uses to touch the lives of His people. When folks come late and leave early, they miss this ministry of the Holy Spirit. It is during fellowship that we learn of each other's life struggles and joys. We connect and thereby strengthen the bonds of friendship. It also informs our prayer life by providing the fuel of compassion needed to lift up the needs of others. It is one thing to hear a request for prayer from the pulpit for a young mother's baby; it is another thing to see the anxiety in her eyes as she describes the problem that threatens her son's health. Texts, e-mails, tweets, and Facebook cannot convey her reality in its full depth. Only face-to-face interaction can accomplish that.

Moving Forward

So, how does a congregation go from a group of self-absorbed people to being a family? That is a strategy best formed at the local level, but there are a few observations that may help. My first observation is: Do not try to fake it. Fake fellowship is worse than no fellowship. At least Simon the Pharisee got that part right. The second observation is that it cannot be forced. The encouragement to "greet three people that you don't know" may be good to break the ice but, in itself, will not engender fellowship. The final observation is, do not give up. Growing fellowship in the flock is a cultural shift not a knowledge shift. It is like spinning a merry-go-round at the playground: it takes more effort to get it spinning than to keep it spinning.

One thing that we have lost as a culture that could aid at growing fellowship is the art of the introduction. When a visitor arrives for the first time, we tend to expect everyone to cold call them. "Cold call" is a sales term that means to try to open a dialog or get a meeting without an invitation or introduction. What if, instead, someone starts by greeting the visitor but before they leave, they introduce that visitor to another person. This forgoes the awkward stage of asking for each other's name and where they are from since that information is passed along during the introduction. As a result, more people feel comfortable connecting with them after the service and possibly extending additional hospitality.

The Shepherd's Goal

One goal of the anointing of fellowship is to open the doors of our hearts to one another. In other words, to take off our Sunday morning mask and be real with each other. Another goal is to provide an identity through acceptance into the family. Our family identifies whom we are, our genetic makeup, and where we belong. Sometimes what happens is that people force their visions of what the family should look like on others. In truth, our spiritual family traits are to be from God the Father. The way that we learn those family traits is the same way a child does, through the interaction with other family members.

In the end, there is no single way to engender a culture of fellowship. The important thing is not to overlook this aspect of the flock of Christ. The goals are to reform the identity of people to that of belonging to Christ and to present an assurance of belonging to each other. In other words, we are first anointed for fellowship by God and then by each other. It is in that place of family fellowship and unity that there is a blessing from God. "Behold, how good and how pleasant it is for brothers to dwell together in unity! It is like the precious oil upon the head, coming down upon the beard, even Aaron's beard, coming down upon the edge of his robes. It is like the dew of Hermon coming down upon the mountains of Zion; for there the LORD commanded the blessing—life forever" (Ps. 133).

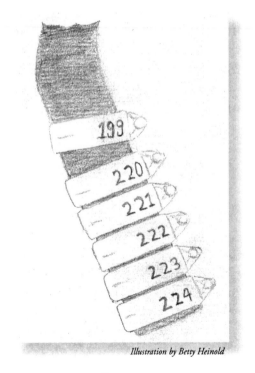

Illustration by Betty Heinold

Ear tags

-13-

My Cup Overflows

The wind shakes the house and the thunder rolls though our bellies. Spring storms can be fierce in central Illinois. They always seem to come in the evening and this one came in fast. On the TV, the weatherman is listing the various warnings and watches for the surrounding counties. Another lightning bolt flashes, lighting the windows. I count out the seconds between the flash and the thunder like Grandpa Kindred taught me. Only three—the storm is getting close. The next bolt causes the lights to flicker for a moment. "Dale, turn to it thirty-one. Let's see what they are saying," Dad says. I get up and turn the knob through the channels of snow until it lands on thirty-one. Another weatherman is running though a list similar to the first channel. Just then, there is a brilliant glow and an instantaneous crack. The lights go off. The only light remaining is a fading small dot from the center of the TV screen. "That one got us; everyone okay?" Dad asks, as he turns on a flashlight he had gathered earlier.

By morning, the power is back on. As we look over the damage, the only visible leftovers from the storm are some downed branches. While we clean those up, Mom comes out and reports, "Duane, we don't have any water, something is up with the well." Dad walks over to the outside hydrant and pulls up the handle. Only a trickle comes out.

"The fuses are okay; I checked them earlier. That one lightning bolt must have hit the well," he says. There is a flurry of phone calls. A well man is secured for the next day. Mom and Dianne head off to Grandpa and Grandma Kindred's. Dad runs to Grandpa Heinold's to borrow the pickup and get a water tank from another neighbor. David and I are left to clean up the sticks and to help Dad when he gets back. After a while, he returns with Grandpa's truck, a filled water tank, and several five-gallon buckets. Dad parks near the back door; he then begins to fill the buckets and gives us our marching orders. David is to dump his bucket in the toilet tank and flush it. I'm to fill the sheep troughs. After lugging several buckets to the barn, I exclaim to Dad, "Those buckets are heavy, I'll be glad when the well is fixed."

"Me too son," he replies.

Our Cup Overflows

King David continues the metaphor of the banquet in which there is so much bounty that it overflows his cup. But what is he trying to say? What is the cup and with what is it overflowing? Since David does not answer these questions, we must turn to the New Testament. John records, "Now on the last day, the great day of the feast, Jesus stood and cried out, saying, 'If anyone is thirsty, let him come to Me and drink. He who believes in Me, as the Scripture said, 'From his innermost being will flow rivers of living water.' But this He spoke of the Spirit, whom those who believed in Him were to receive; for the Spirit was not yet given, because Jesus was not yet glorified" (John 7:37-39). The answer to David's word picture is that the cup is our heart and it is the Holy Spirit that is being poured out by Jesus in such abundance that he overflows. Peter's sermon at Pentecost completes the picture, "Therefore having been exalted to the right hand of God, and having received from the Father the promise of the Holy Spirit, He (Jesus) has poured forth this which you both see and hear" (Acts 2:33). Two things to note from Pentecost are that the Holy Spirit was poured out on individuals and that it happened in the context of gathering.

Let's return to our main question: how is Christ shepherding the church and how can we join in? In some ways, it is fitting that this is the last of metaphor in Psalm 23. So far, we have dealt with twelve "what" pictures, which are the activities and works of Christ in the local body. In this last picture, we arrive at the "how." While we could program our way through the first twelve chapters, the real answer is full reliance on the Holy Spirit to show us the way and to provide an abundance of power to accomplish it. Jesus does not pour out "just enough" of the Spirit, but rather an over-abundance of the Spirit.

Cup Condition

One important question for the local flock is: What is the condition of our cup? Are we prepared to receive that which Christ is willing to pour out? Are we so organized and programmed that there is no room for the Holy Spirit at all? If He desired to change the direction of a life or touch it in a special way, would there be room for it or would it be considered a distraction, an interruption, and a bother? Or, are we so loose that any change is seen as the work of the Spirit even when it is a work of flesh? NASCAR comes to mind for illustrating my meaning. When a racecar is tight, the driver turns the wheel but the car is slow to turn. In some race circles that is called understeer; cranking the steering all the way to the left while the car keeps going straight. The opposite condition is being loose, called oversteer. That is when just the slightest input from the driver causes the back end of the car to break loose, spinning it around. Neither condition is conducive to crossing the finish line. As a church, we need to respond to the input of the Holy Spirit in a way that is in tune with His heart. We need to be sensitive and receptive to the Holy Spirit so that when He corrects our direction we respond but stay within the course He has laid out.

Our cup not only needs to be receptive but it needs to be the right size. Are we ready for the Holy Spirit to touch all of the areas of church? If not, it is like saying to Jesus, "the Holy Spirit is welcome in response to the sermon, but leave our music alone." But Jesus wants to pour out the power of the Holy Spirit on every aspect of church life, from the mundane to the glorious. Does the janitorial crew clean with the power of the Holy Spirit? Sounds silly doesn't it! But that is a ministry alongside all of the other ministries of the body. Do rivers of living water flow out as they clean the floors, or do they complain and grumble at every little mess? The promise is that our cup will overflow, that rivers of living water will flow out. They will, but only in those areas in which we are open to them. The goal, of course, is to be open to the work of the Holy Spirit in all areas of church life.

The Overflow

So, what does the overflow of the Holy Spirit look like? At this point, there may be fear that I'm advocating some kind of emotionally drenched, out-of-control exuberance during the service. While that could be a work of the Holy Spirit (emphasis on *could*), often it is simply the flesh reacting poorly to His power. What does Scripture tell us about the work of the Holy Spirit? I'll be brief. His first and primary work is to glorify Jesus (John 16:14). The second is to convict people of their sins (John 16:8). The Spirit guides us in all truth (John 16:13-14). The Holy Spirit is the seal and assurance of salvation (Rom. 8:14-16). The Holy Spirit empowers our witness (Acts). The Holy Spirit provides gifts of service (Eph. 4:11; 1 Cor. 12:4-11, 28). The Holy Spirit grows the fruit of love, joy, peace, patience, kindness, goodness, faithfulness, gentleness, and self-control in our lives (Gal. 5:22). This list is far from complete but does provide the highlights. The point is that if the Holy Spirit is overflowing in our church these are things we will see. But what if we do not see these works?

Plugged Up Works

The promise is that the Holy Spirit will overflow but our experience tells us that it does not always happen. So, what can stop the overflow of the Spirit? First, we must recognize that it is not a supply problem; it is a receiving problem. The first condition that could stop the overflow is no flow at all, caused by lack of a connection. In other words, everything is done on our own strength, the fuse is blown to the well, and we don't notice or care. The work might get done, but we are the ones lugging the buckets from someone else's well. The second condition is obstruction. The well is flowing but the lines are clogged through neglect and sin. The silt of tradition may also form a clog when we rely on past moves of God instead of how God is moving today. Neglect, sin, and tradition can happen to any church regardless of the age, denomination, or style. Of course, the remedy is to clean those things out. I'm not suggesting the tossing out of all tradition, but rather a willingness to evaluate why we do what we do and make changes as the Holy Spirit leads.

In the previous twelve chapters, there are many suggestions about how Christ shepherds the local flock. It is likely that some of the ideas presented seem daunting, perhaps even impossible. That is where the power of the Holy Spirit comes in. We do not have all of the answers, time, or natural ability needed to carry them out. It simply takes a willingness to join what Jesus is doing, and rely on the power of the Holy Spirit to accomplish the work.

The Pure Bride

In the end, there is no competition between the individual expressions of the local flock. While God will reward our obedience and judge our disobedience, there is only one bride. He is not choosing between brides, He has already chosen her.

The final work of the Holy Spirit is the preparation of His bride. "Christ also loved the church and gave Himself up for her, so that He might sanctify her, having cleansed her by the washing of water with the word, that He might present to Himself the church in all her glory, having no spot or wrinkle or any such thing; but that she would be holy and blameless" (Eph. 5:25b-27). Christ is shepherding His flock in order to complete this vision—and, to put it in 4-H terms, to present a Grand Champion church to Himself.

Two Cheviot Ewes

AFTERWORD

"Surely goodness and lovingkindness will follow me all the days of my life, And I will dwell in the house of the LORD forever." (Psalm 23:6)

No, I did not forget the rest of Psalm 23. While the first five verses present to us a picture of how Christ shepherds His church, this last verse provides a promise for today and eternity.

Christ's Promise for Today

The idea of this phrase is not simply that God's goodness and lovingkindness will passively follow us through life. The picture provided is not one of us pulling goodness and lovingkindness behind us like a trailer behind a truck. Instead, David is fully confident that God's goodness and lovingkindness is pursuing us every moment of our lives. There are two actions hidden by modern translations. The first is emphatic faith. God's goodness and lovingkindness *will* follow. There is no doubt about it. The second is that goodness and lovingkindness do not simply follow but instead are actively pursuing us like heat-seeking missiles.

God is good and desires to pour out good on His people. This is not a promise that all things will be good; notice that it does not say that goodness goes ahead of us and prepares our path. Instead, the promise is that goodness will find us and minister to us in the midst of our today. This thought is brought forward by Paul in Romans 8:28, "And we know that God causes all things to work together for good to those who love God, to those who are called according to His purpose." God does not promise us a life filled with good things, but rather promises that all things, both good and bad, will be used by Him for good and for His purpose in the lives of those that love Him.

The King James translates lovingkindness as mercy. For me that is a reminder that God's mercy towards us is contained in His lovingkindness. God's lovingkindness is found in all that He does for His children: His love, His mercy, His grace, His compassion, His provision, and His discipline. The bottom line is that God will provide for all of our needs according to His rich lovingkindness. That, of course, does not mean provision for our selfish desires. He knows what we need to walk in this world to fulfill the call that He has placed on the church, His people.

Therefore, the promise for today is that God's great goodness and abundant lovingkindness will pursue us as we walk the paths of righteousness for His name's sake. There may be joyous mountaintops and lonesome valleys along that path. Sometimes the path is wonderfully smooth, and at other times covered with sharp stones. No matter how joyful or how painful the path is, at every moment God's goodness and lovingkindness are right there. Often we cannot see God's goodness and lovingkindness in a rocky valley until we get to the other side. Our vision, our focus, is filled with the pain of the moment. But when we look back it will be clear that God's goodness and lovingkindness were there with us all the time.

> I will lift up my eyes to the mountains;
> From where shall my help come?
> My help comes from the LORD,
> Who made heaven and earth.
> He will not allow your foot to slip;
> He who keeps you will not slumber.
> Behold, He who keeps Israel
> Will neither slumber nor sleep.

The LORD is your keeper;
The LORD is your shade on your right hand.
The sun will not smite you by day,
Nor the moon by night.
The LORD will protect you from all evil;
He will keep your soul.
The LORD will guard your going out and your coming in
From this time forth and forever.
Psalm 121

God's Future Promise

David closes the Psalm with a statement of faith and desire, "I will dwell in the house of the Lord forever." That is God's promise for all that call upon the name of Jesus. An eternity of being in the presence of the One that loves us and the One we love. At that time, all will be complete. The church will have become Christ's pure and spotless bride. We will fully see and know the Lord in ways that we cannot begin to imagine. Another Psalm declares that one day in the presence of God is better than a thousand days anywhere else. We can only get glimpses and fleeting moments of that glory at this time. They often come during our quiet times with the Lord or during worship. Some are mountaintop experiences that simply take your breath away at the vista of God's revelation. No matter the depth of our experiences, they are simply a wisp; a sweet momentary taste of what God has prepared for His people.

For God so loved the world,
That He gave His only begotten Son,
That whoever believes in Him shall not perish,
But have eternal life.

APPENDIX A

Victorious Ministry Through Christ

VMTC Prayer Ministry is a means God uses to bring His gifts of the Spirit to bear in the person's life in a deeper fashion while he or she is surrounded by the Love of God. This frees the Fruit of the Spirit to grow and mature in the one receiving ministry (Ephesians 4: 22-24). VMTC lovingly applies the Word of God with Spirit-filled anointed prayer. The sessions are built on a foundation of 150 verses of Scripture dealing with healing, deliverance, and the teaching ministry of Jesus. Each team is composed of one man and one woman ministering together in the unity of the Spirit to "set the captive free."

The VMTC "house-cleaning" session prepares the person to deal more effectively with relationships by removing the "hidden baggage" that cause confusion and loss of focus. This prayer ministry session prevents disruption and distraction from your goal of total commitment. Our focus is not on speed, but on conscientious attention to deal with long-standing problems and relationships. Our prayer ministers are committed to "going the distance" until a new level of lasting freedom is obtained. Some sessions may last 4-5 hours.

Our goal is NOT to solve problems, but to get at the root cause of the problem. While we cannot heal painful memories, we can help heal the relationships so you are no longer enslaved by memories. A VMTC session does not change the circumstance. Rather, it changes people to live victoriously ABOVE circumstances.

We practice what we preach. Each Prayer Minister has received Prayer Ministry at least 3-4 times. VMTC Team Members' training involves "clinical training" with supervision and they must demonstrate they fulfill ministry standards.

The above article from the VMTC website was used with the permission of Victorious Ministries Through Christ USA. Their website can be found at www.vmtc.org.

APPENDIX B

Creutzfeldt-Jakob Disease

Creutzfeldt-Jakob disease, also called CJD, is a brain disorder that causes a rapid decrease in mental function and movement. CJD is the result of a protein called a prion that causes other proteins to fold abnormally. This affects the normal function of the other proteins. CJD is rare, occurring in about one in one million people. There are several variants; the most common is Sporadic CJD, which has an average onset age of sixty-five years old and has no known cause. While the symptoms of classic CJD are like mad cow disease, they are not classified as related. There is a variant that is believed to be directly related to mad cow disease.

GLOSSARY

4-H: 4-H is a youth program begun during the early 1900s in conjunction with the Cooperative Extension Service. It focuses on the various activities of farm life and homemaking. Although aimed at rural youth there is an urban counterpart. The four *h*'s are head, heart, hands, and health.

Alfalfa: A plant related to clover that is cut, sun dried, and baled for winter feeding.

Breeds of Sheep Like other domesticated animals, there is an organized pedigree system for sheep. The breeds themselves vary in markings and purpose. There are wool breeds such as Merino, meat breeds such as Suffolk and Hampshire, and sustenance breeds such as Shropshire. The breeds are named after the region in which they developed.

Cracked Corn: Cracked corn is a simple feed made up of whole kernels of corn that have been put through a press to break the hard shells.

Ewe: A ewe is a female sheep. There are two specific uses with different pronunciations. A young female that has not given birthed is pronounced "you." An older female that has given birth is pronounced "yo."

Feed Sack: A multi-layered large paper sack; when full it weighs about fifty pounds.

FFA: Future Farmers of America is an agriculture-based club for high school aged students. It is a national organization. Its purpose is to train and inform those that desire to work in the agricultural industry at some level.

FFA Jacket: The FFA Jacket is a distinctive blue corduroy Eisenhower-style jacket. On the back is a large FFA emblem, the state and high school in gold letters. The name of the owner is embroidered on the front.

Five high and a tie: This is one of several ways of stacking bales of hay on a hayrack for stability. Five high refers to the levels; a tie is a sixth level only one bale wide that helps to secure the load.

Halter: A halter is generally made of leather straps or rope and fits around the neck and head of the animal. A rope is attached to lead the animal. Animals need to be trained to be halter led.

Hay: Hay is a generic term for dried grasses or alfalfa. In the stories herein, hay refers to bailed alfalfa.

Sheffield Shears: A hand powered device to trim wool. Essentially, they are a simple scissor with a different mechanical design. There are three components. The blades are made of thin steel, wide at the bottom and tapering to a point. Beneath the blades is the handle portion where the operator squeezes to cut. Beneath the handle are two loops of string steel that open the shears when the operator releases pressure.

Straw: Straw is the dried and baled stalks of wheat or oats. It is used for animal bedding.

STUDY GUIDE

Introduction

The purpose of this study guide is to give opportunity to examine where you and your congregation are at in relation to Christ's shepherding. Where sin is exposed, the purpose is for healing. Where success is exposed, the purpose is to glorify Jesus Christ our good shepherd. Our enemy would like nothing better than for this to become a grumble session where all that is "wrong" with the church is chewed over and over. Do not do that! In fact if you are prone to grumble and complain do not do the study at all. For all who are partaking of this study, our attitude must be "look to the log in our own eye first." I give these warnings because the enemy's plan is to dirty the church and make her non-effective. Instead, I challenge you to explore how you and your church can better follow the leading of the Good Shepherd to the glory of God the Father.

Chapter 1

Declaration and Destination

1. What does it mean to own something?
2. What are the rights of the owner? What are the rights of the thing owned?
3. What are the implications of Christ's ownership of us as individuals?
4. What are the implications of Christ's ownership as a local congregation?

The Golden Calf

1. Read Exodus 32:1-8: The Golden Calf.
2. How did the golden calf fall short of what God had revealed about Himself?
3. What are the areas in your life/congregation where one aspect of God's nature is glorified at the expense of another aspect of His character?

Reflection: It is often difficult to see our golden calves until God points them out to us. If you are willing, ask God where and what they are.

Bronze Serpent

1. Read Numbers 21:6-9: The Bronze Serpent.
2. What are the defining moves of God in the history of your congregation/denomination?
3. How does your congregation/denomination interact with past moves of God?

Reflection: Pride is an excellent indicator that an idol is present. Looking back, what events in your life and/or the history of your church have caused pride? Like the golden calf, God will point them out if asked.

Gideon's Ephod

1. Read Judges 8:26-27: Gideon's Ephod.
    a. Exodus 28:6-35 and Judges 17:5 connect ephods with the priesthood.

2. How is this idol manifested in individuals and in the church?
3. Have you ever thought or said that you know better or see clearer than those who have been called to lead your congregation?

Reflection: This is an idol of assumption instead of calling; What activities of your life and congregation have come from an assumption (someone has to do this) versus a calling of God.

Chapter 2

I/We Shall Not Want

1. What does "I shall not want" mean to you and the congregation?
2. What are the basic needs of every person?
3. What are the basic needs of every congregation?

Reflection: Think about times when you determined your needs, when circumstances determined needs, and when you allowed Christ to determine your needs. Reflect on the outcome of each.

Seasons

1. Describe in your own words the attributes of the four seasons.
2. What season are you in personally? Explain.
3. What season do you feel the congregation is in? Explain.
4. Each season presents a different set of needs in addition to the basic needs. What are the needs for your personal season and that of the congregation?

Reflection: How can Christ meet those needs through you?

Chapter 3

The Need to Ruminate

1. After the Sunday sermon, which are you more likely to do:
   a. Discuss what was wrong with the service or sermon.
   b. Forget what you heard and watch sports.
   c. Review and apply what you have heard.

2. How often do you eat to nourish your physical body in an average week?
3. How often do you nourish your spiritual self in an average week?

Reflection: It is important that we not only read God's Word but also take time to ponder, mull on, meditate, ruminate on what it says, and apply it to our lives. How can you rearrange your life to provide this time?

Growing Disciples

1. On a scale of one to ten, how do you handle trouble? One means that I am always in crisis mode, ten means that the house does not even quiver when the storm blows.
2. Would you say that you are a "lamb" or a "mature sheep" in reference to your ability to receive spiritual nourishment?

Reflection: We often do not look back and recognize the labor of others on our behalf. As you do so today, for whom would you want to thank Christ and what did you receive from them?

Feed My Sheep

1. Read John 21:15-17.
2. What is the motive for tending and shepherding?

3. Who does this apply to:
   a. Only Peter
   b. Only the pastor
   c. In some ways all of us

Reflection: While the primary shepherding role in the congregation belongs to the pastor, we all have varying responsibilities both inside and outside of the church. Two things to reflect upon are who is shepherding me, and whom am I shepherding? (Be sure to consider those in the church as well as family, friends, and work.)

Chapter 4

Quiet Waters

1. The chapter indicates that there is not necessarily a connection between the outward atmosphere of a congregation and its peace in terms of relationships; What do you think?
2. Rate your congregation from one to ten in terms of spiritual peace and being family.

Reflection: What can you do to improve the rating of your congregation? Note: this is about you and what you can do, not what others should do.

Troubled Waters—Confusion

1. Read 1 Corinthians 14:33. Who is *not* the author of confusion? Who could be?
2. What actions or events have caused confusion for you during a worship service? Did that confusion aid or detract from hearing the Holy Spirit?
3. The chapter relates that some confusion is from rebellion. Specifically: unforgiveness, perfectionism, people-pleasing, and partiality. What do you think; do these actions and attitudes cause confusion?

Reflection: Of the confusion caused by rebellion, which of these are you most likely to be tempted by? Look back and identify how that action or attitude created confusion for those around you.

Troubled Waters—Distraction

1. Have you ever participated in a perfect service that had zero distractions?

2. Read Hebrews 12:1-2. On whom does the responsibility for staying focused on Jesus lie?

Reflection: Have you ever blamed another for distracting you during church? Reflect on how you can push those distractions aside when they happen.

An additional reflection: The end of the chapter lists several actions and attitudes that may poison the atmosphere: bitterness, disappointment, distraction, rebellion, confusion, untimely words, unforgiveness, judgmentalism, pride, anger, woundedness, apathy, and discouragement. How have you been affected by these? How have you affected others with any of these?

Chapter 5

Restoration

1. What things have you restored from a broken state to a renewed state?
2. Read Luke 15:3-7
3. What are the two emotions portrayed in this passage from Luke?

Reflection: What is your attitude when a sinner repents? What is your attitude when someone repents of the same sin for the seventh time?

Seek Diligently

1. Rate your willingness to seek the lost on a scale from one to ten.
2. Rate your actual actions on the same scale; how often to you intentionally seek the lost?
3. In what ways does your church help you to seek the lost?
4. In what ways could they help you to seek the lost?

Reflection: Looking at the talents, abilities, and gifts that God has given you, think creatively of ways that you could use to reach out to those that are lost and without Christ.

Wash Thoroughly

1. Read Isaiah 1:18, Romans 8:29, and 2 Corinthians 3:18.
2. Have you been washed in the blood of Jesus?

Reflection: Looking back, how has Christ transformed your character from when you first received Christ to today? What character traits is Christ molding in you today? Where do you think Christ may start remolding you in the future?

Cut Off the Residue of the Enemy

1. Read James 1:8; what are the areas in your life where you are "tossed to and fro?"
2. Read James 4:7-8. To whom is James talking? What actions are we to take?

Reflection: How have your past experiences, your sin, and the sin of others affected your walk with Christ?

Note: Once you have identified an area of bondage, of residual impact in your life, how do you deal with it? There is not enough space to cover that fully in this study guide. The major parts are to confess, repent, receive forgiveness, and renounce your sin. The subsequent part is to forgive those that are involved. That will bring cleansing. However, there may be "dingleberries" remaining that will need to be removed through spiritual warfare such as that offered by VMTC.

Chapter 6

Paths

1. Read Psalm 84:5-7. Looking back over your walk with Christ, how has your life changed?
2. What do you think the psalmist means by "strength to strength?"

Reflection: Which paths in your life are easier to walk in righteousness; which paths are the hardest for you?

Righteousness

1. Read Micah 6:8. What does the Lord require?
2. The chapter states that righteousness should be something we are, not simply something we possess. What are your thoughts about that and how would it change your walk?
3. Consider the Pharisees; they acted righteously but were they righteous in reality? Why were they, or why were they not?

Reflection: Where are your "dark corners"—the places in the life that are not righteous before God and man?

Guide

1. Whose walk do you see as a model to follow?
2. People are following our walk whether we know it or not. What kind of example are you being for others?
3. What is your expectation of the example of leadership?

Reflection: What are the parts of your walk that you hope others see and emulate? What are the parts that you hope that they do not see and would be ashamed if they followed?

Our Guide

1. Even though we follow the walk of others, who is our ultimate guide?
2. Read Mark 13:21-22. What are the false christs in the world today?
3. Read Matthew 16:24-25. What is the cost of following Christ?

Reflection: Consider the cost of following Christ. In what ways are you following your own way instead of the way of the cross?

Chapter 7

Why Do We Do?

1. Read Isaiah 26:8.
2. Think about how often you talk about your church and its activities in relation to how often you talk about Jesus.
3. Where are you on a scale of one to ten, where one is "here mostly to receive" and ten is "here mostly to give?"

Reflection: Even if you rated yourself as a ten, what more could you do to bring glory to Jesus?

Questions for Leaders (and everyone else)

1. List some of the recent decisions that you have needed to make.
2. How did you make those decisions? What criteria were important to you in arriving at you conclusions?
3. Is there a decision in your past that you know now you should have decided differently?

Reflection: Concerning making decisions, think of what your habits currently are. Think and pray about which habits need to be set aside and replaced with new ones that will lead to decisions that glorify Jesus.

The Judgment

1. Read 1 Peter 5:1-4 and Colossians 1:28.
2. How are you doing in reaching the standard seen in these verses?
3. Read Colossians 3:17. What of the things of life are we to do for Jesus?

Reflection: The standard is high, whatever you do . . . do all in the name of the Lord Jesus. What things of your life do not bring honor and glory to Jesus?

Chapter 8

The Church and Loss

1. How does your church deal with loss?
2. How comfortable are you in dealing with someone that has recently experienced a loss?
3. If you have experienced a loss, what were your feelings concerning how the church and the church family responded?

Reflection: The chapter lists several suggestions to improve response from and care by the church family for those who have experienced loss. Which ones do you feel you need to improve?

Jesus Knows the Pain

1. Describe the comfort Christians have in regards to death.
2. How could you comfort someone going through loss?
3. Have you ever taken "fine" for an answer?

Reflection: The church often does well in the first few days of loss. First, reflect on what your church does during the first few days. Second, think about how the church interacts with a loss after three weeks and after six weeks. How could the church's response improve? Do not limit your thinking to what the leadership could do but consider the church family as a whole.

Additional reflection: Tell your own story about a loss that you have experienced.

Chapter 9

We Fear No Evil for You Are With Us

1. Read Psalm 27:1 and Romans 8:33-39.
2. What can separate us from the love of Christ?
3. What are the things that come against your faith in Christ?

Reflection: Have you ever felt separated from Christ? Think about that time. How did that feeling begin and how did it end? If you feel today far from Jesus, recognize that Jesus is not far from you and reflect on what may be causing your feelings.

Fear

1. What do you fear?
2. Consider the three responses to danger. Which are you most likely to do? Which are you least likely to do? Why is that?

Reflection: Consider the difference between reaction and response. The first is our automatic action to the moment; the second is the prayerful action to the moment. Think about how to change from reacting to responding to the situations of life.

Wisdom

1. Read James 3:13-18. How does he describe natural wisdom? How does he describe heavenly wisdom?
2. Read James 1:5-8. How is godly wisdom acquired?
3. What is the beginning of wisdom?

Reflection: Think about the fear of God and evaluate your walk with God in relation to the complementary aspects of love and fear.

Chapter 10

The Shepherd's Rod and Staff

1. Read Hebrews 12:6.
2. The rod speaks of both discipline and authority. Recount an instance when you encountered the discipline of God's rod.
3. The staff provides safety and support. Recount an instance when you felt God giving you strength and balance through a difficult time.

Reflection: Evaluate your receptiveness of the correcting hand of God.

Comfort

1. List some things in which you find comfort.
2. Describe the heart of the shepherd toward the flock.
3. Does the knowledge that the goal of disciple is to encourage healthy growth bring you comfort?

Reflection: Think about God's view of your comfort and consider your own view. Which one do you think will bring the most growth in your walk with Christ? In what ways could you change your thinking concerning comfort and the Christian walk?

The Pastoral Role

1. Make a list of the expectations you have for your pastor.
2. Consider your pastors: What are their weak areas; what are their strengths?
3. What on your list of expectations, could others supplement in the flock of Christ?

Reflection: If you are a pastor or leader, how could the flock support you or supplement the needs of the congregation? If you are a member of the flock, how could you support and assist in meeting the needs of the others in the congregation?

Chapter 11

The Banquet

1. Read Revelation 19:9 and Isaiah 25:6.
2. Recall a banquet that you attended. Describe the event, the decorations, and the celebration.
3. What do you think that marriage supper of the Lamb will be like?

Real Enemies

1. Read Ephesians 6:12. Describe these enemies: what are their goals; what are their methods of attack?
2. Read 2 Corinthians 12:5. Describe this enemy: what are its goals; what are the methods of attack?
3. Read Hebrews 12:4. Describe this enemy: what are its goals; what are the methods of attack?
4. Read Romans 8:37. How are we victorious against these attacks?

Reflection: Ephesians declares that our struggle is not against flesh and blood. Consider also Jesus words in Matthew 5:43-45. Reflect on ways to defeat the enemies of sin, the world, and the devil while still loving the men and women through whom those attacks come.

Winning the Battle

1. Think about your prayer life. On a scale of one to five, one being seldom and five being often, rate the time spent in the following areas of prayer: worship; intercession for others; intercession for yourself; thankfulness; confession; giving and receiving of forgiveness; waiting and listening. Looking at the numbers, in what area(s) should you work to improve?

2. Think about your time with God's Word. How often, during the week, do you spend meaningful time interacting with the Word? Quality is better than quantity; how can you make your time in God's Word be of better quality?
3. Read James 4:7. Whose battles are you fighting, yours or Gods?

Reflection: Warriors spend a great deal of time polishing, sharpening, and improving their skills with their weapons. How could you improve in the areas of prayer, the Bible, and humility?

Chapter 12

The Anointing

1. Read Luke 7:36-50.
2. When you have invited guests to your house for a celebration, how do you greet them? What are other common ways to greet people?
3. In this context, the anointing has the purpose of welcome and acceptance. How do you feel when you are welcomed into someone's home?

Welcoming Hospitality

1. How does your church welcome guests?
2. Whose responsibility is it to welcome guests and regular attenders? Whose responsibility should it be?

Reflection: Think of ways that you can improve when meeting, welcoming, and showing hospitality to guests and regular attenders.

The Shepherd's Goal

1. Read Psalm 133.
2. Considering the church, whose family is it? Where then should the family traits come from?
3. Describe how God has welcomed you into his family.

Reflection: Describe what the outcome would be if the brothers and sisters of your church fully loved and accepted each other in unity and love of God.

Chapter 13

Our Cup Overflows

1. Read John 7:37-39. To whom does John equate "rivers of living water?"
2. Thinking over the last twelve lessons, what change that you reflected on is the most challenging or impossible for you to accomplish?

Cup Condition

1. Rate your feelings about being open to follow the Holy Spirit from one for "scared silly" to ten for "bring it on." Explain why you rated yourself that way.
2. Are their areas of your life that are "off limits" to the Holy Spirit? What are they?
3. Apply questions 1 and 2 to your church.

Reflection: Think about you and your churches willingness and openness to the Holy Spirit. What are some concrete steps that can be taken to achieve a better balance in order to run the race to the end?

The Overflow

1. This section contains a list of the works of the Holy Spirit.
   a. To glorify Jesus, John 16:14
   b. To convict of sin, John 16:8
   c. To guide into truth, John 16:13-14
   d. To seal and assure, Romans 8:14-16
   e. To empower of witness, Acts
   f. To provide gifts for service, Ephesians 4:11; 1 Corinthians 12:4-11, 28
   g. To grow fruit in us, Galatians 5:22

Reflection: Reflect on this list. Which of them are easiest for you to accept, which are the hardest?

Plugged Up Works

Reflection: The Holy Spirit always desires to pour out more than we can contain. If your cup is not overflowing, consider which of the two causes the issue is. Is it a matter of not being willing to receive? It is a matter of sin? While many sins could plug up the works, the most common and the most difficult to remove is the sin of pride. Reflect on the issue of pride in your own life and in the life of the congregation. God's Drano of confession, repentance, and forgiveness is powerful and can remove even the toughest clog.

The Pure Bride

Final reflection: Think about Paul's description of the bride of Christ in Ephesians 5:25-27. This is Christ's vision for the church. Reflect on how that vision can become reality in your life and the life of your church.

Contact the Author

The author can be contacted through his website www.lambchow.com for questions, comments, and speaking engagement requests.